THE LIVERIES OF THE PRE-GROUPING RAILWAYS

VOLUME ONE

WALES AND THE WEST OF ENGLAND

FLYING DUTCHMAN

THE LIVERIES OF THE PRE-GROUPING RAILWAYS

VOLUME ONE

WALES AND THE WEST OF ENGLAND

NIGEL J.L. DIGBY

Lightmoor Press

Designed by Nigel Nicholson

British Library Cataloguing-in-Publication Data.
A catalogue record for this book is available
from the British Library

ISBN 9781 911038 28 3

LIGHTMOOR PRESS

Unit 144B, Lydney Trading Estate, Harbour Road,
Lydney, Gloucestershire GL15 4EJ

www.lightmoor.co.uk

Lightmoor Press is an imprint of
Black Dwarf Lightmoor Publications Ltd

Printed in Poland; www.lfbookservices.co.uk

ESTABLISHED 1856.

Contractors for MORE THAN HALF A CENTURY to the whole of the principal British, Indian and Colonial Railways, and to the Indian and other Governments, &c., &c.

TEARNE & SONS, Limited,

All Saints Road, BIRMINGHAM.

Original Manufacturers of

TRANSFERS

FOR

RAILWAY CARRIAGES, LOCOMOTIVES, TRAMCARS, &c.,

ARMS, MONOGRAMS, WRITING.

Every Description of Inside & Outside Ornamentation, Notices, &c.

Telephone : Central 237. **Telegrams : "Tearne, Birmingham."**

White lead, an essential material in all railway paint shops, being manufactured and packed in barrels at the Glasgow factory of Alexander Fergusson & Co., who were preferred suppliers of colours to the Caledonian Railway. As well as specialising in the production of white lead, the company also produced a full range of colour paints. *Neil Parkhouse collection*

Contents

The Volumes

When this collection was first published in *British Railway Modelling*, it appeared four times a year. In order that readers could count upon a railway from their area being covered at least once a year, I allocated each of the companies to a point of the compass; West, North, South, East in that order. To give an idea of my thinking, the first four paintings I executed were in order Midland Railway, North British Railway, London & South Western Railway and Hull & Barnsley Railway.

When addressing the subject again, I considered using the Grouped railways as the key to each volume. However, this made some volumes rather heavy, and others very light. To resolve this I returned to the geographical area idea, but this time with a few alterations. The result was a more balanced table of contents for each volume.

Volume One is 'Wales and the West of England', Volume Two 'The East and North-East', Volume Three 'The North and North-West', and Volume Four 'London and the South'. There is still a preponderance of railways from each appropriate group, for example the GWR in this volume, but now with interlopers from other groups included simply because they are in the right geographical area.

Wagon painters at work in the paint shop of the Gloucester Railway Carriage & Wagon Company circa 1925, applying one of several coats of lead colour, which were standard under all wagon finishes. *Neil Parkhouse collection*

Barry Railway van No. 653, photographed at Gloucester in December 1902, just prior to delivery. Note the distinctive cast-iron Gloucester Railway Carriage & Wagon Company builder's plate on the left-hand end of the solebar. The van is painted in brown oxide livery with white lettering, as detailed on page 20. *Courtesy Gloucester Archives*

Introduction

I have always been much more interested in the railways that existed before the Grouping of 1923 than those that came after, and these paintings are the direct result of an article I did in 1993 for David Brown, the first Editor of *British Railway Modelling* magazine. It was about the Eastern & Midlands Railway, for which I did a painting of an E&MR locomotive. David thought it could be the prototype of a complete series. Commencing in 1994, the list of paintings in the series that I planned to do stretched out before me for an unimaginable length of time. The paintings, and the articles accompanying them, appeared quarterly in *BRM* for twelve years.

The formidable list I compiled of forty-eight livery articles covering forty-four railway companies was a leap into the unknown. Time and time again, when moving on to yet another company, I wondered if this would be the one that would defeat me, but somehow something always turned up. This was no accident, because behind the great many casual railway enthusiasts there is a small band of dedicated and intelligent researchers who discover and record the real facts behind their particular railway, and whose assistance I received gratefully.

Before 1st January 1923 there were nearly fifty standard gauge steam-powered railway companies possessing their own stock in Great Britain. Each had their own distinctive livery, sometimes changing it several times during the life of the company. Increasingly, railway modellers, enthusiasts and commercial manufacturers are looking at these companies, and it is of the utmost importance that they get the liveries right.

To reconstruct a livery accurately requires a variety of sources, the more contemporary the better. The task can be immensely difficult, principally because the prime sources are frequently absent. Many of the specifications written by the railway companies themselves have been lost. It seems surprising now, but few people in the post-Grouping era were interested in preserving the memory of the old companies. It was not really until the 1950s that groups of enthusiasts such as the Historical Model Railway Society began to gather together reliable references. Other than official records, the next prime source would be from the railwaymen themselves but, incredibly, until the recent rise in interest in oral history, the testimony of these men was often ignored. The historian usually has to fall back upon secondary sources. Fortunately, eye witness accounts were printed in the contemporary press, some by reliable authors, but the bulk were supplied by enthusiasts (or 'railwayacs' as they were called) out on the platform. Unfortunately, some of these railwayacs had a rather eccentric way of describing colour.

In any statement involving colour, random factors intrude: the individual's colour perception, the circumstances under which the colour is viewed, and the surface condition of the coloured object. Defining a colour is therefore a very subjective process, and is almost impossible unless some part of the original formula is known. It is easy to see, therefore, that a great cause of confusion has been the naming of different colours. Apparent conflicts arise which are resolved when one realises that different names are the responses of different people to the same colour, often with a subjective connotation such as 'grass' or 'olive' when describing a green, for example. In fact, some quite ridiculous names were used by uninformed observers (and by some who should have known better) and all of them were fond of using potentially misleading shorthand terms, for instance the words 'lake' and 'teak'. Later writers in turn put their own interpretation on these secondary sources, usually incorrectly, creating a whole raft of myths and misinformation which, unless challenged, become accepted as fact. In other words, an awful lot of bunk has been written about railway liveries, and it is in the spirit of cutting through the dross to get at the facts that this series of volumes is written.

The National Railway Museum is usually regarded as the prime modern-day source of colour information. Indeed, useful colour patches have been produced using the panels companies often prepared on which to mount their so-called 'coats-of-arms'. However, not even being part of the National Collection guarantees authenticity. A case in point is the Great Eastern Railway livery. The GER locomotives at the NRM were allegedly matched to a surviving sample of the Stratford oil colour found in a tin, but over time this dried fragment had darkened considerably, and its application ignored the effect of a transparent pigment over a pale grey undercoat. Great Eastern blue was very much brighter than that which the near-black appearance of these engines would suggest.

In fact the early preservationists made many mistakes when painting their newly-rescued locomotives. Perhaps the worst example of false authentification is the preserved Highland Railway 'Jones Goods' 4-6-0, which has been painted in a bright yellow ochre colour alleged to have been used for a short time when the engines were new. To use this transitory and almost certainly apocryphal livery on an engine which should rightly carry the standard Jones green is to my mind one of the biggest scandals of railway preservation. Frustratingly, because these finishes were applied over fifty years ago, they have in their turn become 'historic', and there does not seem to be any chance of repainting any of these abominations into a correct appearance any time soon.

Another common mistake made by the preserved railways is to use modern single-coat paints and wonder why the final result is not quite what they expected. The reason is that they have ignored the profound effect that the many coats of varnish had on the locomotives or carriages in their original state. Modern paints do not give the wonderful deep shine of copal varnish, nor do they age or weather in the same way.

When researching liveries, the only other record of colour comes from contemporary postcards and paintings such as those in the *Railway Magazine* and *The Locomotive*, although these can only be used as a confirmation of a style rather than a precise reproduction as printing tends to vary from batch to batch. Ordinary black and white photographs are also valuable as evidence of lining styles, and (with careful examination) as indicators of certain colours too. Unfortunately, although relative tones of different colours and the junctions between them can often be distinguished, the old 'colour-blind' or orthochromatic photographic emulsions are unreliable when gauging the actual colour value. These emulsions were insensitive to red, and very sensitive to blue. Thus red areas such as bufferbeams come out very dark, and skies are invariably blank white. This frequently makes any vermilion lining all but invisible. The later panchromatic plates or films, which would have given better colour rendering, were not used very often by railway photographers.

Once the correct colours have been determined, the time that each was used has to be assessed. Very often only a general date of adoption or abandonment can be given, there being no official record of a particular change to be found. Usually this does not matter overmuch. When railway companies changed their colours or styles it did not happen overnight. There would have been a considerable time lag in the adoption of a new livery before all examples were dealt with. Sometimes, if changes were particularly rapid, some engines or vehicles may miss out on the first change altogether, going straight from their original condition to the final condition.

An interesting phenomenon made apparent by the overall study of railway liveries is the fact that before 1880, almost all railway companies painted their locomotives green of one shade or another, and were devoid of company initials, relying on numberplates to show ownership. Similarly, although passenger vehicles often carried some initials or at least a device, goods stock was usually completely unmarked save for a number, or perhaps a symbol.

Then in the 1880s there was a sudden burst of activity. Almost every company changed at least its locomotive livery in that decade and started applying company initials to wagons, although few of them were large at this stage. I do not know why the companies suddenly indulged in this orgy of colour. It may be that the new industrially-produced chemical pigments were a cheaper alternative, or they may have been prompted by commercial considerations, in an attempt to make their railway stand out from the others as a sort of advertising campaign. The Furness Railway is recorded as taking precisely that road when changing its carriage livery to blue and white, in order to attract more tourists to its district. There was another movement for change in the years 1903-1906, when many Victorian styles were simplified and large letters became general on goods stock.

At the other end of the era, many railways adopted plainer liveries during the First World War, and restoration to the old styles after the war was slow or abandoned altogether. Thus, although the title of the series collected here uses the expression 'pre-Grouping', I have set myself the more specific parameters of between the years 1890 and 1914, when the railways were at their zenith.

As can be gathered from this introduction, railway liveries are complex and fascinating, and make an ideal subject for colour treatment. As far as I know, my series of articles was the first serious attempt at a comprehensive study of pre-Grouping railway liveries that included carriages and wagons as well as locomotives. Naturally, the size at which the paintings in these volumes are reproduced is many times smaller than the real thing, and the exact colours cannot be used, even if the printing process allowed it. As a small area of colour is perceived as darker than a large area of the same colour, the shades used in the paintings are slightly lighter than those actually employed.

Where possible, the colours are given references. The first (Carter) is from the colour chart in E.F. Carter's *Britain's Railway Liveries*. This book is essential to anyone serious about railway liveries, although when the paragraphs of text are compared with the original sources from which they are taken, many errors of transcription or interpretation are found. Nevertheless, the colour chart was built up from examples of sample panels and backgrounds for armorial devices prepared by the railways themselves, now in the National Collection, and seems to be mostly correct with a few anomalies. The second reference [Pantone] is from the Pantone PMS formula guide, particularly useful for the print media. The third [BS] is from the British Standard colour charts of which there are several. BS 381 was first issued in 1948 for special paints in public buildings and for the military. A more comprehensive chart of 237 colours, BS 5252, was issued in 1976 for all building materials, from which BS 4800 makes a selection for paints. I have not included Munsell references as it is almost impossible to get physical access to a Munsell chart, whereas the other three are readily available second-hand or new from online auction sites. Sometimes it is not possible to get an exact match. Rather than interrupt the flow of the text, the colour references are shown as endnotes to each company. For example, the reference for M&GN locomotive colour [1] is shown at the bottom of this page.

The sources of information consulted were many and varied, as described above, but I have relied heavily on the work of the societies that have sprung up over the past twenty years or so, dedicated to the study of almost every railway company. Detailed acknowledgements are given as an appendix. I am grateful to Neil Parkhouse for sourcing new photographs, and these, with further colour sketches, paintings, contemporary postcards and colour patches, make this collection different from what has already been published. I have also revised some paintings and their text according to further information received. The final sparkling result is due entirely the skills of designer Nigel Nicholson.

1
'LIGHT BROWN'
CARTER 32
PANTONE 1395
BS 5252 08 D 44
OR BS 381 410
'LIGHT BROWN'

Painting Methods

As my research into pre-Grouping liveries commenced, I found that only a minority of sources, such as the HMRS's excellent *LSWR Livery Register*, were able to quote exact figures of paint proportions or relative weights of colour used, and far too often I was forced to use references from the past and the present which used relative terms. It rapidly became obvious to me that I would have to go back to first principles, to look again at the actual mechanics of painting railway stock. What also became clear was the ignorance of most commentators, past and present, of the actual practice in the average railway paint shop, leading to the promulgation of many myths and much misinformation. Here I found myself in an advantageous position, because not only was I acquainted with two men who had once been employed in the paint shop of the Midland & Great Northern Joint Railways at Melton Constable, I had the writings of others reproduced in the *Bulletin* of the M&GN Circle.

Almost every railway company had its own paint shop, from the large ones at Derby and Crewe dealing with thousands of locomotives, carriages and wagons, to the more modest ones such as Melton Constable or Highbridge, dealing with hundreds. On a normal railway (excluding those paralysed by lack of money) in the period before the Great War, locomotives and rolling stock were dealt with regularly. This meant that an engine would return through the works (depending on mileage) on average every three years, receiving greater or lesser attention to the boiler and other parts as was required. Almost invariably, the locomotive (and tender) would be repainted at the same time. It was vital to keep this protective layer unblemished, not just from an appearance point of view, but also to prevent deterioration of the metal underneath. The damage inflicted on paintwork by the weather, boots, fireman's tools and minor mishaps can often be seen on photographs.

Carriages and wagons were also meant to return to the works for attention every three or four years, although this was probably given a greater amount of flexibility, their treatment being less rigorous than that of the locomotives. What happened to them in the paint shop would depend on their state at the time. From remains I have been able to examine of M&GN carriages, it seems that a full repaint occurred on alternate visits, that is, after six or seven years. In the interim, it is likely that a touch-up of worn areas and lettering sufficed, with a full rub-down and revarnishing. For goods wagons, remains indicate a full repaint on every third visit to the works, after about nine or ten years. This explains why there were still some pre-Grouping wagon markings around on the grouped railways ten years after the event.

A paint shop one hundred years ago was little different to one today, needing the same parameters to function properly. It had to be clean, well-lit, well ventilated and kept at a steady temperature. During the colder seasons, the temperature was maintained by hot water pipes to at least 60 degrees Fahrenheit (15 degrees Celsius), in order that the fillings, paint and varnish hardened. Ventilation was crucial to avoid condensation, which interfered with the paint surface, and to avoid the build-up of fumes. Lighting was provided by windows or skylights, ideally facing north to avoid direct sunlight. Internal walls and roofs were painted white to increase reflected light. It can be appreciated that the painting of railway stock, particularly of locomotives, was a rigorous and involved process, not to be undertaken lightly. This, as Lyn Brooks pointed out in the *Great Eastern Railway Journal*, explodes such myths as

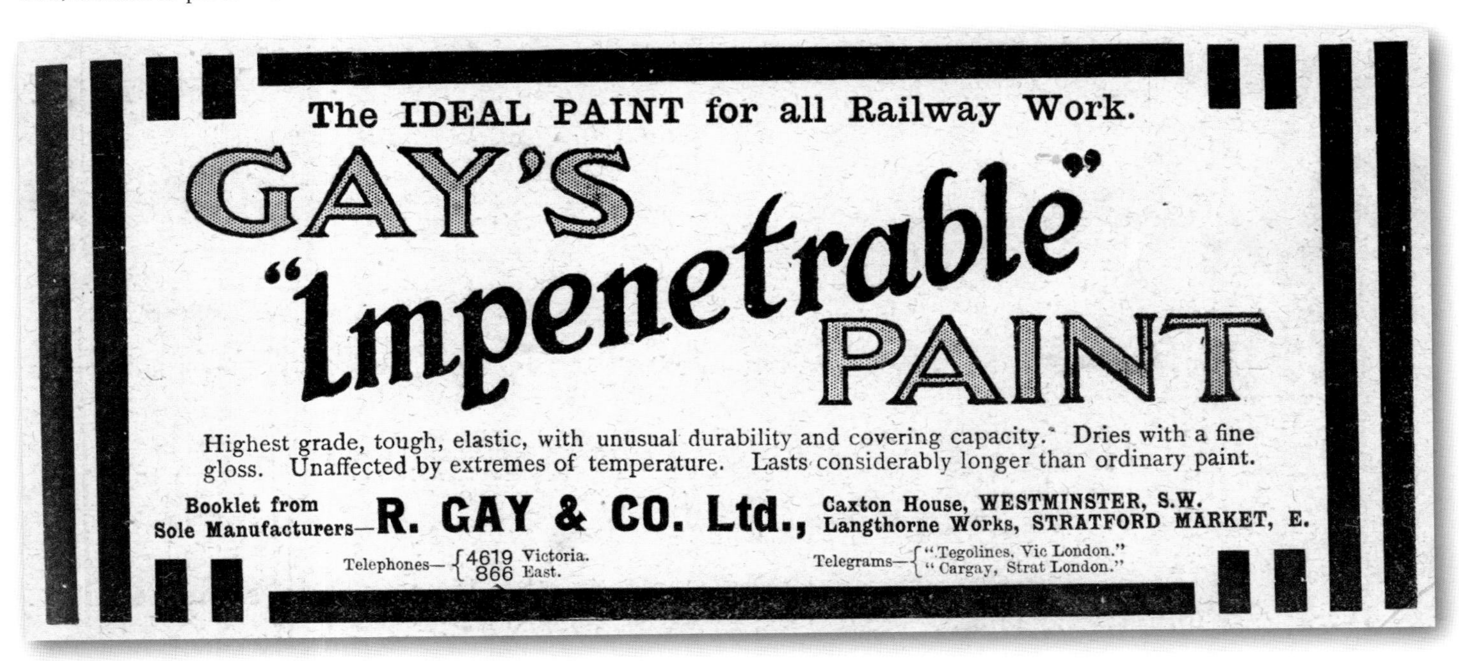

'Cambridge blue', where GE engines were supposedly repainted at the Cambridge shed in a lighter version of the ultramarine blue. This is only one of the myriad examples of misinformation that become absorbed in the public's consciousness and are very difficult to dislodge, particularly when commercial outlets pander to them.

As an independent entity until being brought under the control of the London & North Eastern Railway in 1936, Melton Works managed to preserve almost all aspects of the pre-Grouping railway into living memory, and as such is a valuable window into the past. Although only small, Melton can be taken as a microcosm of any railway works, and the carriage & wagon department to be typical of any in the British Isles. In overall command was the carriage & wagon shop foreman. Under him was a little community of coach builders, wagon builders, carriage trimmers, leather workers, stores men, wheelwrights, pattern makers, vacuum fitters, machinery operators and labourers. But the most important members of the department from our point of view were the highly-skilled painters, who also executed the intricate jobs of lining, carriage graining and fixing of transfers. There were five painters, of which one was senior, and four apprentices, who did much of the menial work whilst being trained in the various skills and techniques.

In the paint finishing shop were the stores of paint, varnishes and solvents. It must be remembered that until comparatively recently, oil paint was the rule, applied by brush. Paint of the necessary quality was not available in handy tins, ready to apply, in the way we are used to today. It was bought in bulk and had to be prepared before use. The pigments arrived from the suppliers in two forms: paste and powder. The paste was in large drums, and had to be rendered into usable paint by the addition of turpentine (genuine, not the substitute) and linseed oil. The mixing bench had flat surfaces on which to mix putty or filler if need be, and was provided with a hand paint mill. This machine mixed the ingredients to render the paint usable. It was a laborious process but always gave a perfect result. Large paint shops such as the one at Horwich (Lancashire & Yorkshire Railway) had several powered mills and mixers.

Some of the more expensive pigments arrived as powder in chamois leather bags. The process for these was even longer, requiring the powder be ground into a paste with linseed oil and gold size first, before thinning with turpentine into a usable paint. Varnish and gold size, being consumed in considerable quantities, were kept in large tanks. Some of the big paint shops used agitators in these tanks to prevent deterioration. Turpentine was also used in large quantities, as it was essential not only in the thinning of paints but also in the drying process, enabling the item being painted to receive a coat a day. The smell of all these paints, turpentine and varnish, not to mention the pungent odour of freshly-worked teak coming from the carriage shop next door, must have been wonderful.

A comprehensive glossary of the materials used in the typical railway paint shop is given in the next chapter, to which the reader should refer throughout the following paragraphs.

Locomotives

As a 15-year-old apprentice in 1928, the late Charlie Porter once told me that he was not allowed even to paint bufferbeams, let alone anything more intricate. Among his first tasks was to go to the erecting shop, where the locomotives were disassembled, and paint the motion, big ends, cranks and axles of the wheels while they were easily accessible. These were given two coats of vermilion and varnished. Once the locomotive had been mechanically finished, it was sent to the paint shop. Some railways prepared at least one side of the engine in light grey, lined out in black and white, so that it could be photographed. On occasion, locomotives were completely finished in grey, lined, lettered and varnished and sent out on running-in turns to see how they behaved. This was not the practise at Melton, and the running-in turn to Fakenham and back was usually done in full livery.

On getting the engine and tender into the paint shop, all loose paint and grease was removed, and any bare metal given a coating of 'lead colour' (grey). Lead colour was universal to railway paint shops, being cheap to make and protective of the metal. This was rubbed smooth and then the whole engine given a coat of lead colour. All holes, scratches and dents were filled with 'stopping', and then three coats of brush filler were applied. This was rubbed down to a perfect smooth surface using pumice blocks, taking two men and two boys a full two days.

Once rubbed down, a priming coat of lead colour was applied. What followed varied from railway to railway, depending on the final colour of the engine. Those companies using an 'opaque' colour, such as green, now simply applied three coats of that colour. Others, such as the Midland, the Great Eastern, and the M&GN, whose final colours were achieved by the use of a transparent colour over a coloured undercoat, differed slightly. The GER utilised a very pale grey, which they sometimes called 'aluminium', over which they then applied three coats of ultramarine blue. The pale undercoat shone through, ensuring a bright and sparkling final result. The Midland employed two coats of iron oxide or 'purple brown', over which the final coat of alizarin crimson mixed with a little oxide was applied, giving a red of great depth and lustre. The M&GN painted two coats of yellow ochre, over which a final coat of the transparent raw sienna was glazed, giving the 'autumn leaf' shade.

Other parts of an M&GN engine were also painted at this time. Bufferbeams had two coats of vermilion, as did the inside faces of the frames. The lower parts of the engine were painted in three coats of burnt sienna. The smokebox had a coat of drop black and then a coat of black japan, an acid-resisting varnish. A cheaper brand of black, known as vegetable black, was used on brake gear and other less visible parts under the engine. Cab interiors were often a lighter colour, and on the M&GN the upper parts were painted buff and then grained to look like wood. Other railways preferred plain buff or cream but, in contrast, the engine-builder Beyer, Peacock & Co. used vermilion. Jimmy Platten, the senior painter at Melton, did all the graining, both in the cabs and on the carriages.

Once the final coats had dried, boiler bands were painted in drop black, and the black lining and edging elsewhere on the engine was applied, before the first coat of varnish. Once that had dried, the lettering transfers and fine lining in lemon chrome could be done. Lining was a skill that elevated the best painters to the level of artists. Straight lines were achieved by 'snapping' a stretched string covered in chalk, and chalk was also used with a straight edge. The quarter-inch lines were applied using 'pencils' and 'swords', which were specially-shaped brushes. A young painter would learn this process by being allowed to line something less important, such as a horsebox.

The lettering and insignia for any company were almost invariably transfers supplied ready-coloured. This was useful for particularly intricate shading, such as that on the Midland-type transfers that the M&GN used, or later on the lettering of the L&NER. However, at Melton when stores had temporarily run out, Jimmy Platten could do them by hand.

After the lining and lettering came a further two coats of varnish. Some railways could exceed this, for example the Midland employed five coats in the 1890s. The engine then had to stand for three or four days to harden off. All in all, the whole process could take up to three weeks, and this is just for one engine.

On the M&GN at the end of the 1920s, in common with other railways, economies had to be made and locomotives were given much less preparation. Stopping was much reduced, and the rubbing-down of filling abandoned. Dark brown was adopted for all engines, one coat applied over the lead grey primer, followed by one coat of half paint, half varnish. The M&GN lettering changed to large yellow characters, painted by hand. Their shape was placed on the surface of the tender by another paint shop technique, the use of pinpricks through a drawing and a chalk dust bag. There was one finishing coat of varnish.

The method of using a top coat of half paint, half varnish had been used by some companies for many years, and was referred to as an 'enamel'. It had the advantage of being self-levelling and avoided brush marks. It became more common to receive colours as ready-mixed enamels of this type, such as L&NER locomotive green, and lining tended to be used only for the more important units. During the Second World War and after, patch-painting was increasingly used as a way of protecting the material beneath without going to the expense of a full repaint.

Carriages

Carriages were finished according to the type of timber in which they were clad. The internal framing of the vehicle was usually American oak, although teak could be employed, with softwoods such as red fir for the boarding of roofs and floors. The carriages were panelled with sheets of hardwood, typically ⅜ of an inch thick, the joints between panels being covered by beading of the same hardwood.

The majority of British railway companies opted for mahogany for their cladding, which was usually painted, the wood taking paint well. The exception was the London, Brighton & South Coast Railway, who apparently varnished their mahogany. For painted carriages, there was first a regime of stopping and filling and rubbing down before two or three coats of lead colour. On top of this the company colours were applied. Three coats seem to have been the rule, the top coat often being the half paint and half varnish 'enamel'. The Midland, having the transparent alizarin crimson to cope with, started with one coat of 'lake ground', which was probably the same red-brown iron oxide used on the engines, one coat of crimson lake, and one coat of 'lake and varnish', another example of an enamel.

On top of the base colour, the beading, if it was a different colour, would now be painted, and then the whole secured by a coat of varnish. After flatting down, lining and lettering followed, before three or four coats of varnish, flatted down and washed between coats. The top coat was always the hard-drying 'finishing' varnish, which gave that mirror-like shine common to all freshly-painted carriages.

About a quarter of the total number of railway companies decided to clad their carriages in the more prestigious and durable teak. This left them with a problem, as teak is a very oily wood and does not take paint well. M&GN painter Frank Morgan told me that the secret was to start with one coat of best gold size, which acted as a sealant and a base for the subsequent coats of varnish. Any holes were now filled with coloured putty, and any light-coloured panels treated with a stain to give a more uniform appearance. There then followed one or two coats of varnish, flatted down with pumice and washed between coats. At this point, the lining and lettering would be applied, followed by another three coats of varnish, again flatted down between coats, with the finishing varnish topmost.

Some railways adopted a 'painted and grained' finish. On the carriages inherited by the M&GN from its predecessor, this was done to deceive the passenger, the vehicles being clad in mahogany, but painted and grained to look like teak. However, the more usual reason was to replace a varnished wood finish which had become unsightly after ten to twenty years of exposure to the elements. Its application was one of the most skilful talents possessed by the paint shop. Using the M&GN carriages as an example, they were first rubbed down, filled and stopped in the usual manner. Then followed two coats of lead colour, the first one thinned with turpentine. On top of the lead colour were two or three coats of the ground colour, which was meant to be slightly lighter than the lightest components of the depicted wood grain. For teak, the M&GN chose 'buff'. This was based on lead white, mixed with yellow ochre and Indian red to give a deep, pinkish cream. Over this were the graining coats.

The method chosen by Jimmy Platten at Melton was to use water colours bound with stale beer (from the Hastings Arms) and thinned with rainwater. This was known as 'distemper graining'. Painters in other railway paint shops may have used the alternative 'oil graining'. Mr Platten's mix involved raw and burnt umber, and raw and burnt sienna. Because the graining colour dried quickly, he would have had to work at one panel at a time. The close graining of teak would have been simulated by drawing graining combs and stiff brushes down the length of the panel, possibly followed by 'figuring' with a rag over the 'veining horn' or a thumbnail. Once dry, the initial graining was finished off by 'overgraining' with a special brush having separated bristles, then the edges softened with a badger hair brush. A coat of varnish secured the graining before the application of lining and lettering. There followed two or three coats of finishing varnish in the usual manner.

Carriage underframes or solebars could be of oak, but with the increase in length of bogie carriages, steel became the material of choice, or at very least a steel cover or 'flitch plate'. Steel would first be treated with anti-corrosive paint (red lead) but thereafter the method was the same as for timber. After a coat of lead colour, there followed four coats of filling and stopping, rubbed down to a smooth finish. The work was then given another coat of lead colour. The solebars of painted coaches were then given one coat of the body colour, one of the enamel body colour, and one coat of varnish. However, as time went on, the universal choice for solebars became drop black.

It was the custom for teak carriages (and those painted and grained), after the same preparation noted above, to have solebars painted with three or four coats of teak colour, and one coat of varnish. An unusual practice followed on some railways, namely the finishing of the metal boltheads, footboard brackets and buffer casings in 'bronze green'. This appears to have been the use of a special varnish on top of green paint. The varnish was prepared from shellac and had suspended within it the bronze powder. To prevent tarnish, the bronzing layer was quickly treated with one or two coats of finishing varnish. The Cheshire Lines Committee, and by extension the Manchester, Sheffield & Lincolnshire Railway, used this technique on the entire solebar.

Carriage roofs were constructed from tongue-and-grooved boards of red fir following the contour of the roof supports. The boards received one coat of lead colour, and all joints and screw holes were properly stopped. One good thick coat of white lead was then applied, on which the canvas roof covering was bedded and tightly stretched, and secured at the cornices. Some railways now followed with three coats of white lead, but others opted for lead colour.

Wagons

Many wagons in the earlier period were built entirely from American oak, solebars and underframes included, although some builders preferred jarrah for these members. This was a hard and heavy timber of the eucalyptus family imported from Australia. Timber underframes were given one or two coats of lead colour.

As time went on, it became increasingly normal for wagons to have steel underframes. These would be given two coats of anti-corrosive paint. Some companies opted to 'pickle' parts of their steel underframes, which would be immersed in a bath of sulphuric acid solution for half an hour, then neutralised in an alkali bath before being washed, dried and painted with two coats of graphite paint.

The entire wagon was now given two coats of lead colour. Some companies applied a final coat of lead colour and left it at that, employing grey as their company colour, but others used reds, browns or dark greys, and these were applied in one or two coats over the lead colour. Lettering was painted on in white, and ironwork such as buffer casings or body strapping (if required) 'blacked' using black japan. Varnishing was not generally used on wagons, which left them more at the mercy of the weather. It was not unusual for wagons painted red oxide to fade in the sun until they were almost pink.

Wagon sheets

Sheets (never called 'tarpaulins' by the railways as far as I am aware) were of variable size, but usually in the range of 21 × 16 feet. They were machine-sewn from thick brown canvas in special workshops. Brass rings or eyelets were let into the edges at regular intervals for fastening cords. Under normal circumstances, these were all that were needed to attach the sheets to the fastening rings on the wagons. Larger loads would require the use of ropes, and probably more than one sheet. A high load of hay would need three.

Once sewn, the sheets were painted with vegetable black. In some works this was done by the simple expedient of laying the sheets on the floor and going over them on both sides with special painting brooms, making sure the canvas was thoroughly soaked through with the oil colour. In others, a dipping process in a vat of the paint was employed.

After painting, the company initials and a unit number were added in white lead, using a stencil. Some paint shops completed each character or number after the stencils were removed, others didn't bother, leaving the visible gaps caused by the stencil paper. Further identification was sometimes provided by coloured stripes or symbols. A few companies also marked the back or reverse side of the sheets, particularly at the corners.

So we come to the present day, separated by 100 years from the pre-Grouping period, and we return to the perennial question: just what colour do we paint our models? I would extend that to include preserved items, as the problem is very similar. In many ways one could say that a preserved line is simply a model railway writ large. I would recommend going back to first principles. Don't just take the word of 'experts' like me, I urge you to try things for yourself. It simply involves a trip to your local art shop to buy oil paint (artist's quality if possible) and turpentine, a palette knife and something to mix on. Follow the processes set out in these volumes and watch the colours appear. Allow a little lightening with white, because small models look too dark with the true shade of paint on them, and only then you will be in a position to judge whether that expensive tin of paint you bought for your locomotive, carriage or wagon is really the right colour.

Materials in a Typical Railway Paint Shop

During the period under consideration (c.1890-c.1914), almost all paints and varnishes used were oil-based. Oil paint consists of a finely-ground pigment mixed with a binding medium, usually linseed oil. This solidifies in contact with air, holding the particles of pigment suspended within it. Depending on the pigment, oil colours may be transparent, semi-transparent or opaque, and vary in cost. Transparent colours were used as a glaze over a coloured undercoat. Several liveries exploited the depth given by this technique, therefore being impossible to reconstruct except as an approximation in any other medium.

However, it is not wise to be too pedantic regarding railway colours, for the very reason that oil colour was the medium used. It is not inert, and responds to its environment in a variety of ways. Under the strenuous conditions of day-to-day running and cleaning, the pigments matured and changed, some fading, others darkening. In addition, the effect of varnish is always underestimated. In the several layers common to painting practice in pre-Grouping days, its yellow colour had a profound effect on finished liveries, turning white into cream, yellow into orange, and light blues into light greens. On passenger rolling stock it was meant to deteriorate and be replaced regularly without need for a full repaint.

Great reliance was put upon having an adequate base for the livery – locomotives and carriages having a long process of stopping, filling and rubbing down to a billiard table standard of finish. The last preparatory treatment was the application of a coat or two of primer, usually 'lead colour' (grey) or 'iron oxide' (red-brown).

For the main company colours, the chargehand painter would be in charge of the mixing process, and relied on weighing out the pigments, his expert eye, and matching to prepared colour boards to arrive at the correct paint. Some would have you believe that this led to great variation in the paints derived. Even the NRM in its *Liveries Resource Pack* falls into the trap of assuming that, just because these methods were employed over a century ago, they and the pigments used were therefore unreliable. As far as I am concerned, this is nonsense. These highly-skilled men knew exactly what they were doing, and any significant variation would not have been tolerated by those in charge.

Below are the common paints and other materials to be found in a typical railway paint shop. Some of these colours are still available as artist's oil colours today, but because of the regulations surrounding the use of lead and other poisonous products, only non-poisonous equivalents are available in the average artist's materials shop.

Black Pigments

Almost all commercial blacks were made from carbon obtained by calcining organic material. Calcining was the process of cooking in a closed oven with a controlled amount of oxygen. The best grade used in paint shops was drop black, a bluish black with a name derived from the shape of the lump in which it was originally delivered. The equivalent artist's oil colour today is ivory black. A cheaper pigment, vegetable black, was used for unimportant areas such as brake gear. Black japan was a black varnish made from asphalt. Being acid-resistant, it was commonly used on smokeboxes, and sometimes on the iron strapping of goods wagons.

White Pigments

Almost all paint shops used white lead exclusively. This was manufactured from basic lead(II) carbonate and was also known as flake white (not to be confused with the L&NWR carriage 'flake white'). An opaque, brilliant white with very good covering and mixing properties, it darkened to brownish grey when exposed to sulphurous air. Being poisonous, it is hard to obtain in the present day and the usual commercial equivalent is titanium white. A few railways preferred zinc white (zinc oxide), particularly for carriage roofs. A brilliant white, but rather transparent, it did not darken so much on exposure to sulphurous air. It is often sold today as mixing white.

Grey Pigments

Invariably these were a mix of white lead and drop black in a variety of tones. The lighter end of the range was usually referred to as lead colour or lead grey. The Great Eastern used an exceptionally light lead colour on locomotives and sometimes referred to it as aluminium.

Red Pigments

This colour had a huge range and could be produced from chemicals or naturally occurring substances, which tended to cross over into browns.

Lakes were paints created from pigments which only existed as liquid dyes, absorbed into an alumina base. Alizarin crimson was a transparent crimson lake made from a coal-tar derivative. Introduced in 1868, it replaced nearly all of the older natural red lakes, for example madder, made from the root of the madder plant. One natural red that persisted was carmine, a crimson lake made from cochineal, a dye extracted from a tropical beetle. A rather fugitive colour, it was violet-crimson in hue when fresh, but faded over time to allow more of the undercoat colour to show through.

The Victorian equivalent of high-visibility paint was vermilion (mercury(II) sulphide), a brilliant orange red, often applied to bufferbeams and the motion between the main frames. Another poisonous pigment, today one can usually only obtain a 'hue', made from cadmium red.

The iron oxide series of reds was based on iron(III) oxide. A range of shades were available. The darkest of the oxides was purple brown. This was originally manufactured from calcined yellow ochre (see below) and in this form could be named colcother. Otherwise, it was often made in paint shops by mixing Indian red with black. Purple brown was a warm crimson brown with a slight violet hue. However, in the railway press it was an indiscriminate and unreliable term. Indian red, also known as red oxide, was a red-brown colour with a slight blueish cast. A lighter red-brown was Venetian red, which was iron oxide with a large proportion of clay containing calcium sulphate. The lightest form was light red, the most scarlet pigment of the iron oxide series. This was originally manufactured by the calcining of yellow ochre to a lesser degree than purple brown.

Chocolate was a term used indiscriminately by contemporary observers to describe reds and red-browns which to modern eyes bear no resemblance to the eponymous substance. The Midland Railway called Venetian red 'chocolate'. It is too imprecise to be recommended for serious use.

Brown Pigments

This group of paints includes several derived from natural earths. Starting at the redder end, and derived from iron oxide, was brown oxide, which had added manganese dioxide as a colourant. Also at the red end was burnt sienna, manufactured by calcining the natural earth raw sienna, to produce a transparent rich red brown.

Of the true browns, raw umber, a natural earth containing iron and manganese, was a cool, dark greenish brown. It was apparently sometimes referred to as 'Quaker green', possibly also a name used for raw sienna. The warm, darker brown of burnt umber was produced by calcining raw umber.

Yellow Pigments

An early yellow was yellow ochre, originally a natural earth containing iron hydrate. It has a complex colour, with green and brown constituents. There were some sources of the pigment in this country, Oxford ochre being one. Later it was manufactured from the oxidation of iron(II) sulphate. Iron Hydrate is iron(III) hydroxide or, more correctly, hydrated iron(III) oxide, a natural constituent of both yellow ochre and raw sienna, although the name could be used in its own right. Raw sienna was another natural earth containing iron hydrate and manganese. It was similar in hue to yellow ochre, but browner and more transparent.

The first manufactured yellow appeared in the early 19th century. Chrome yellow was lead(II) chromate. A large variety of shades, from the pale lemon chrome to the deep orange chrome were produced by varying the method of manufacture. The usual commercially-available equivalent today is based on non-poisonous cadmium yellow.

Blue Pigments

Ultramarine was a brilliant, slightly reddish blue. It was originally made from lapis lazuli and was very expensive, but from 1828 was manufactured and sometimes known as French ultramarine or royal blue. A duller alternative was Prussian blue, iron(III) hexacyanoferrate(II), a deep, greenish blue, first introduced in 1724. Both blues tend to be transparent in oil. Brunswick blue was Prussian blue extended with barytes (see below). The name referred to the quality rather than the colour.

Green Pigments

The usual green used in railway paint shops was chrome green. This was an intimate mixture of Prussian blue and chrome yellow, manufactured simultaneously in the same vessel. A great many shades of green could be produced, but railways tended to simplify things and used shades often referred to as 'light', 'middle' or 'deep'. They should not be confused with modern chrome or chromium green, which is chromium(III) oxide and was originally known as 'viridian'. Brunswick green was a chrome green made from Brunswick blue and chrome yellow, again capable of considerable variation of shade, also known as Prussian green. It was a cheaper grade of paint than pure chrome greens, rather than a different colour. Olive green is an imprecise designation used for any number of mixtures, but usually applied to chrome greens turned slightly by the addition of small quantities of black and white.

Extenders

To make paints cheaper, and to allow them to be less transparent and cover greater areas, extenders were sometimes used. The natural form was called barytes, which was mostly barium sulphate. The manufactured form was called blanc fixe. The extenders had some 'body' and would inevitably slightly lighten the hue of the paint to which they were being added.

Gold

Gold leaf was used for lining, affixed with gold size, a glutinous substance not unlike varnish. It could also be used for lettering, but more frequently transfers of lettering were provided already gilded.

Teak

Varnished teak became rather a cliché among contemporary observers, taken up by modern commentators. Any form of varnished wood was referred to as 'varnished teak', despite the fact that there was no guarantee the wood was indeed teak, and ignores the frequently-used technique of railway paint shops to paint and grain carriages. Teak colour was a reddish brown paint supplied ready-mixed, also known as 'solebar brown' and used to simulate the colour of the varnished wood. Its shade varied considerably between batches and companies.

Varnish

This was invariably an oil-based copal varnish, which possessed its own yellow colour, particularly when applied in several layers, as was the custom. It gave a hard, glossy shine, but it turned considerably darker with age and could crack.

Enamel

This term was applied to oil paint which had an equal proportion of varnish mixed with it. It was advantageous in being self-levelling, eliminating brush marks.

Turpentine

A volatile solvent distilled from the resin of certain pine trees. It thinned and accelerated the drying of oil paints so that a coat a day was possible.

Linseed Oil

A light oil pressed from flax seeds and refined using sulphuric acid. It was used as a vehicle for pigments and as a medium for further thinning when mixed with turpentine.

Barry Railway

The Barry Railway was incorporated in 1884 to build a dock at Barry, seven miles west of Cardiff, and over twenty miles of railway to serve it. The company was promoted because the Bute Docks in Cardiff were unable to expand to handle the increasing coal traffic of the district. The main line from Barry to Trehafod (near Pontypridd) on the Taff Vale Railway was opened in 1889, giving access to the great Rhondda Valley. In the 1890s a policy of expansion was instituted, beginning with Barry Island in 1896, then westward to the Great Western Railway at Bridgend in 1897, eastward to the Rhymney Railway (1901) and finally to Barry Junction on the Brecon & Merthyr Railway (1905). By 1906 the length of line was only 66 miles, but by virtue of the junctions with the TVR, RR and B&MR the Barry had access to nearly all the collieries in the Glamorgan coalfield.

Although mineral traffic was the chief reason for the Barry's existence, the company also ran a heavy suburban passenger service in and around Cardiff. At first passenger trains ran only as far as Cogan (near Penarth Dock), but by dint of agreements and link lines with the GWR and TVR, the company was later able to run into Cardiff (Riverside) and Bute Docks (Clarence Road). There were also passenger services to Porth in connection with the TVR, and Bridgend in connection with the GWR.

The company's offices were next to Barry Dock station, and the locomotive, carriage and wagon works at Barry Town. The works were able to rebuild and repair locomotives and rolling stock, but all locomotives were built by outside contractors, mostly Sharp, Stewart & Co., to the specifications of Mr J.H. Hosgood, the first Locomotive Superintendent. In 1905 he was succeeded by Mr H.F. Golding, and then in 1910 by Mr J. Auld.

The Barry became a constituent of the Great Western Railway in 1923, and passed into the Western Region of British Railways at Nationalisation in 1948.

The base colour of Barry locomotives was a dark crimson brown [1], described in sources as being dark lake, dark brown, dark red, red-lake or red-brown, or dark crimson lake. Some researchers have taken from this the assumption that the colour got redder as time went on, but there is no real basis for this conclusion as many railways liveries suffered the same variance in description. A surviving specification states "chocolate – as sample", which is typically unhelpful.

Tanks, bunkers and valances were edged with black, and boiler bands were black, all fine-lined vermilion [2]. Tanks and bunkers were lined in a broad black band, which in the 1890s was fine-lined on each edge with yellow, but thereafter with vermilion. Wheels were dark crimson with black tyres and axle ends, lined vermilion. The engine numbers were placed in brass numerals on the chimney

Barry Railway 'K' Class No. 120, one of a class of five locomotives built in 1899 by the Cooke Locomotive & Machine Works of Paterson, New Jersey, USA. The engine is in Barry livery with the second style of numberplate, but has no device.

Neil Parkhouse collection

Barry Railway

fronts and on the rear of the bunkers. Four of the locomotive classes (Class 'C' 2-4-2T, Class 'E' 0-6-0T, Class 'G' 0-4-4T and Class 'J' 2-4-2T) were considered 'passenger' engines, and were fitted with polished brass domes and safety valve bases. Their chimneys were capped in brass, and polished brass fillets were fitted between smokeboxes and boilers.

All engines were identified with large brass numberplates. On the locomotives built before 1892, this plate carried seriffed numerals over which was simply the word "BARRY". From 1892, engines appeared with a second, more conventional, plate on which the number was surrounded by "BARRY" above and "RAILWAY" below. All plates were polished brass on a black background.

The device was applied to all engines – usually on the bunker, but where maker's plates made this position impossible, on the cab. This varied from engine to engine between the lower cab and the upper side in front of the cab cut-outs. The first device consisted simply of an elliptical garter surrounding the entwined script letters "BR". The garter carried the words "BARRY RAILWAY COMPANY".

Bufferbeams were vermilion, edged with black and fine-lined white. Buffer casings were lined at lip and base. As the number appeared elsewhere, front and rear bufferbeams carried the lettering "B [hook] R" in gold, shaded in blue to the right and below.

The only Barry engines with tenders were the four Class 'D' 0-8-0s. Their brass plates were on the cabsides. Earlier tender lettering was "B R" in widely-spaced letters of the same type as on the bufferbeams with the first device on the sandbox, but a later photograph shows "B [device] R" on the tender, featuring the second device (see below).

Mr Golding introduced a number of changes in the 1905-10 period. On rebuilds a third style of numberplate appeared on which very large numerals were surmounted by a small "BARRY RAILWAY C^{O}", and the date placed below. A new device also appeared. This second device consisted of a Welsh dragon surmounted by a stag's head crest, surrounded by an elliptical ribbon bearing the lettering "1884 BARRY RAILWAY COMPANY", the date being split on each side of the stag's head. More noticeably, several engines were

now lined out in broad bands of green, fine-lined with yellow. Mr Golding also began removing chimney numbers and placing them on the bufferbeams, for example "N^{O} [hook] 88".

From 1910, Mr Auld reversed some of these changes. Lining returned to black and vermilion, although goods locomotives were now unlined. Where brass chimney numbers had been removed, a small polished steel numberplate was sometimes fixed in their place. However, the Class 'L' 0-6-4Ts of 1914 carried their numberplate on the smokebox door. Another change occurred during the First World War: although a few shunting and goods engines already had their coupling rods painted vermilion, during the war most engines received vermilion rods, which they retained until Grouping.

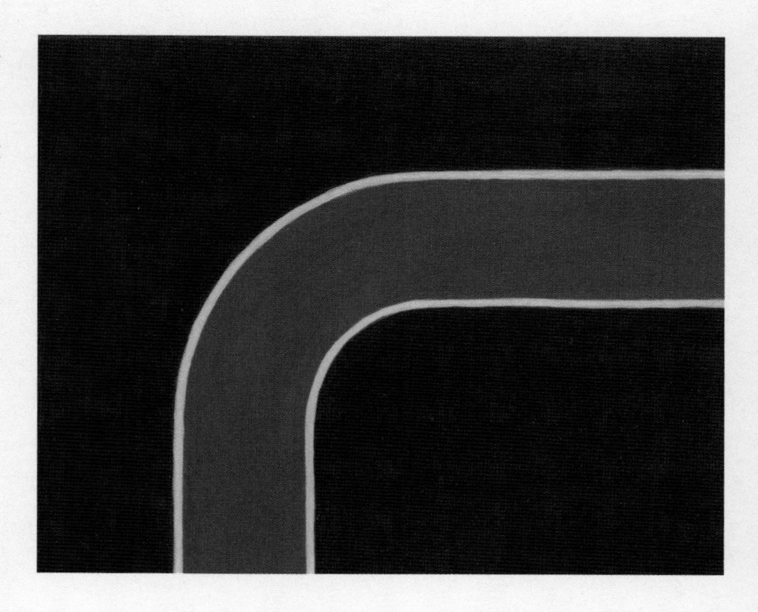

RIGHT: Mr Golding's lining applied 1905-10 to several engines.

18
Barry Railway

Carriages were painted the same dark crimson brown as the locomotives [1]. Beading was painted black, lined in gold. Carriage ends were unlined. The new bogie coaches of 1920 had an unusual body styling, not lending itself to the standard lining, and so these were lined in gold (or yellow) only. Carriage solebars were painted black and roofs were white when new.

Lettering was in gold sans-serif characters. The main lettering was about 3 inches high, and was arranged in a symmetrical fashion on the waist panels. The vehicle number was in the panels between the end compartments, the device being placed below each. The company initials "B.R" were on the next panels within. Class marking was in words, "FIRST", "SECOND" and "THIRD", the characters being about 2 inches high. Other door lettering used was "GUARD" and "LUGGAGE COMP^{T}".

There is some doubt over the shading colour. It seems that the carriages originally had red shading, but this was subsequently

changed to blue, both with white highlights and shadowed in black. The date of changeover is unknown and is the subject of further research by the Welsh Railways Research Circle.

The 1920 bogie carriages were lettered in a different style. The symmetrical arrangement was preserved, but the numbers were small and the second device was placed under the initials instead. Class marking was in large seriffed numbers on the lower door panels, a style which may also have been applied to older stock as it went through shops. The style is said to have been introduced by Mr Golding, but photographs seem to contradict this, only being seen late in the life of the railway.

Goods vehicles received 'three coats of Stevenson & Davies brown protective paint' according to a specification of 1890. This is almost certainly what was known as brown oxide [3], a warm, brownish red. The ends of brake vans were vermilion [2]. Photographs of the brake vans in traffic suggest that the verandah doors were vermilion

Barry Railway

as well. Body ironwork was picked out in black japan. All below the solebar was black.

Lettering was in white characters, possibly with black shading to the right and below. Open wagons had "BARRY [door] C^O" in the middle of each portion of the side in 6½-inch letters, with "N^O" and the number below in 6-inch characters. Load was usually painted on the right-hand bottom plank, "LOAD 10 TONS" for example, with the tare next to it. Vans had the same lettering, but its position was high up and near each end of the vehicle. The number and its prefix were placed on each leaf of the doors. Brake vans featured the "BARRY C^O" lettering in the upper part of the side with the device positioned centrally below. The number, with prefix, was positioned on either side of the device, for example "N^O [device] 47".

There were other lettering arrangements observed. One incorporated all the lettering along the top plank of open wagons, possibly an earlier form, and another used "B^Y C^O", which may have been one of Mr Golding's ideas.

From about 1909 all former styles were replaced by a bold "B R" in plain white letters up to about 24 inches high. Numbers were to the lower left, and also on the lower plank of each end. Brake vans had the number in a larger size than normal, placed centrally on each side, and also on the left of each end. Brake ends and verandah doors were vermilion.

Wagon numberplates were rectangular with incurved corners, and carried "BARRY R^Y C^O" over the number. Wagon sheets are also reported as being lettered "BARRY C^O", with three red bars.

Large goods lettering.

1
'Dark crimson brown'
Carter 27
Pantone 1817
BS 381 449
'Light Purple Brown'

2
'Vermilion'
Carter 36
Pantone 485
BS 5252 04 E 55
or BS 381 536
'Poppy Red'

3
'Brown oxide'
Carter 30
Pantone 4695
BS 381 490
'Beech Brown'

Brecon & Merthyr Railway

The Brecon & Merthyr Tydfill Junction Railway, to give it its full title, extended from the busy ports of South Wales to the wilds of the Brecon Beacons. It was essentially in two sections, northern and southern, separated by a short stretch of the neighbouring Rhymney Railway. At the southern end it served Newport, Caerphilly and Rhymney, and came into intimate contact with the Barry, Rhymney, Alexandra Docks and Great Western railways. The northern section ascended steeply from Pant and Dowlais to Brecon, where it shared its station with the Neath & Brecon, Cambrian and Midland Railways. South of Pant the B&M was primarily a mineral railway, but north of that point was a steeply-graded rural line with a sparse passenger service. Its total mileage was 61½ miles.

The origins of the B&M could be said to extend back to 1826 with the opening of the Rumney tramway from the ironworks at Rhymney down the east bank of the river to Bassaleg near Newport, or even further back to 1816 when the Hay Tramway was opened from Brecon, sections of both of these later forming part of the system. However, the B&MR proper was established in 1858, opening its first section from Brecon to Pant in 1863. In the south, the B&M purchased the Rumney, acquiring that tramway's running powers into Newport. The conversion of the tramway into a standard gauge railway was completed in 1865, but remained separate from the northern section. Before a link line could be opened, a legal obligation to finish a branch to Merthyr had to be fulfilled. The contractors Ward & Savin, who had also worked the line, had failed in 1866, leaving the Merthyr line unfinished. It was eventually opened in 1868, freeing the B&MR to complete its link line and arrange running powers over the Rhymney Railway. Brecon to Newport trains began on 1st September 1868.

The company's works were at Machen, inherited from the Rumney company, where the superintendents in more recent times were Mr G.C. Owen (1888-1909) and Mr James Dunbar (1909-1922).

The Brecon & Merthyr became a constituent of the Great Western Railway in 1923, and passed into the Western Region of British Railways at Nationalisation in 1948.

Like many smaller railways, the B&M received scant attention from contemporary 'railwayacs'. The locomotives were covered to some extent in the railway press, but rolling stock was all but ignored; the most complete entry in livery terms is one printed as part of a series by *The Locomotive Magazine* in 1897. In the B&M's case the problems are compounded by two further difficulties: one was that the staff rarely cleaned anything; the other that there seems to have been a marked reluctance to repaint anything after delivery from the makers or, in the case of secondhand stock, the former owners. The result is that the few photographs that exist show such dusty and faded stock that it is impossible to see any livery features at all.

Locomotives have been variously described as being painted brick red, lake, or bright red, and as far as is known had been so since the

Brecon & Merthyr Railway No. 3, one of a class of twelve outside-framed 0-6-0STs built in 1884-86, in the standard post-1890 livery. Note the lining taken over the integral cab roof and the home-made windshield. *John Alsop collection*

Brecon & Merthyr Railway

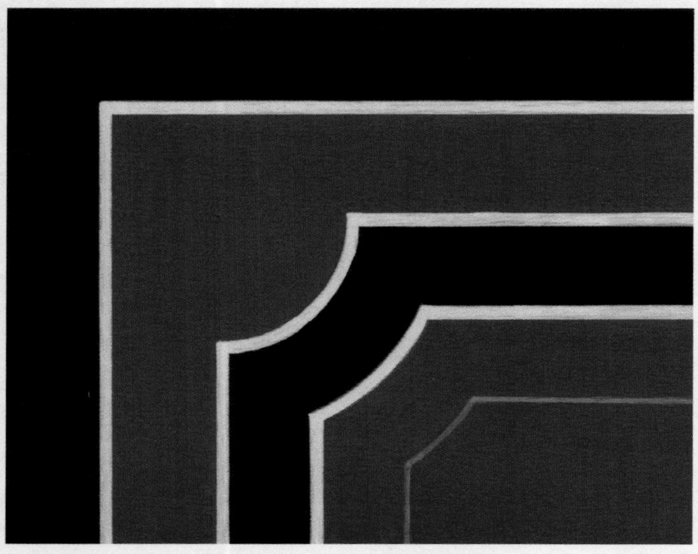
Original locomotive lining.

start of the line. The colour was indeed quite a bright red-brown [1], apparently Venetian red, one of the iron oxide series. Lining until circa 1890 was quite elaborate, consisting of each panel being outlined in black, including each tender panel and each section of any saddletanks, fine-lined in yellow. Inside each of these panels was further lining in black with incurved corners, also fine-lined in yellow on each side, and reportedly with a further line of vermilion a short distance within. Incidentally, although the B&MR owned several tender locomotives in earlier times, tank engines, and particularly saddletanks, were found much more satisfactory and the last tender loco, *Usk*, was converted into a tank engine in 1895.

From about 1890 Mr Owen simplified the livery. The body panels were now only edged in black, fine-lined yellow, with an inner fine-line of vermilion. Boiler bands were black, edged in yellow. Wheel tyres and axle ends were black, lined yellow, and there was a black and yellow line around each wheel centre. Smokeboxes, footplates and inside frames were black, although outside frames were the body colour. Cab roofs were also black, except where the roof was integral with the side, as on the 'No. 1' Class 0-6-0ST,

Brecon & Merthyr Railway

when it was body colour. Inner faces of frames and bufferbeams were vermilion [2], the latter being edged with black and yellow. Brass domes were fitted to many of the engines, and these were polished, as were the safety valve seatings and also the brass cleading between the smokebox and boiler of the 2-4-0T passenger engines.

The only sign of ownership was the elliptical brass numberplate, bearing "BRECON & MERTHYR" over and "RAILWAY COMPANY" under the central number, on a vermilion background. Bufferbeams had the number painted on in the usual manner, "N^{O} [hook] 17" for example, in yellow shaded in black, although in many photographs the bufferbeam is so dirty it is impossible to distinguish the characters.

This remained the state of affairs for most engines until the First World War, with one notable exception. A new class of 0-6-2T locomotives began arriving at the end of 1909, and it seems there were some differences in their livery, although it is impossible to say whether these changes applied to all twelve of them or only to the eight delivered from 1914 to 1921. The B&M Venetian red was superceded on these engines by a darker red-brown, noticeable

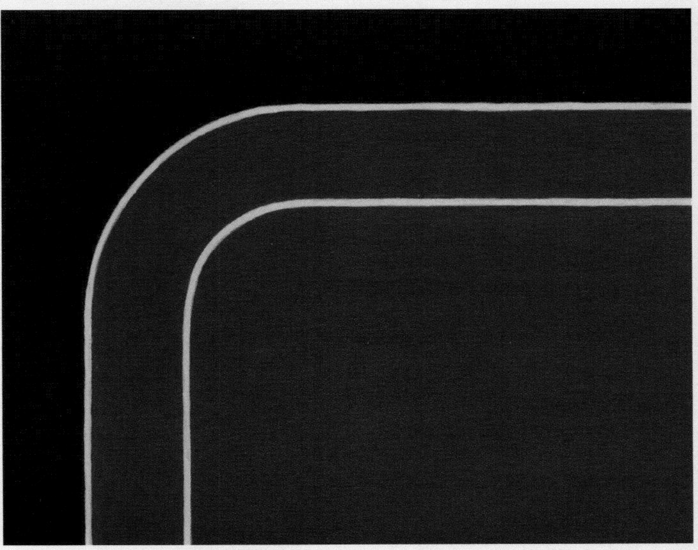

Lining of the 'chocolate' engines.

Brecon & Merthyr Railway

Brecon & Merthyr Railway No. 31, built by the Avonside Engine Co. in 1874, apparently seen here in the wartime plain black.
John Alsop collection

Brecon & Merthyr Railway No. 44, built by Beyer, Peacock & Co. in 1879 for the London & South Western Railway. Lining is faintly visible on the body and boiler bands; the body colour is the subject of conjecture.
John Alsop collection

Brecon & Merthyr Railway

Brecon & Merthyr Railway No. 11, built by Robert Stephenson & Co. in 1889, in the standard livery with polished dome.

John Alsop collection

Brecon & Merthyr Railway No. 43, built by Robert Stephenson & Co. in 1914, on the turntable at Brecon. This was one of the so-called 'chocolate engines' with non-standard lining.

John Alsop collection

enough for the local children to call them the 'chocolate engines'. The lining was still confined to a black edge with a yellow fine-line, but now the inner line was also yellow. There was no polished brass except on the numberplate. The bufferbeams were edged in black only.

There were other exceptions to the usual livery. During the First World War, several of the 'No. 1' Class 0-6-0ST were painted black. A number of engines were obtained secondhand from the GWR and these remained in the GW unlined green. An ex-London & South Western Railway 4-4-2T was obtained in 1914 and, whatever its livery originally, it was turned out from Machen in 1922 in 'crimson lake'. Quite why this was done, or whether indeed this is a true record of its colour, has never been satisfactorily explained. It may well be a typical railway press mis-statement and the engine was merely finished in the standard red-brown.

If understanding the liveries of the locomotives was difficult, understanding that of the carriages is almost impossible. Most of the stock built for the B&M which survived into the 20th century dated from the 1881-1894 period, almost all built by the Metropolitan Carriage & Wagon Company. From 1903 only secondhand vehicles were obtained, from the Mersey, Metropolitan, London & South Western and Midland railways. It seems that very little work was done on the secondhand carriages, and their treatment may account for some of the conflicting reports of the carriage livery.

When delivered new, it is almost certain that the B&M carriages carried a purple brown body colour, very similar to that of the London & North Western [3]. Lining was apparently gold or yellow fine-lined vermilion on the edge of the beading, with a fine white line actually on the panel itself. Lettering was "B&MR" in the waist on one side with "N^{o} [number]" on the other, in gold or yellow, shaded in red and black. Class marking was in words on the waist of the door, and three classes were used. The company did possess an armorial device but there is insufficient evidence to say that it was used on anything but the saloons, two on each side. There was also

a script monogram of "B&MR", placed centrally on the saloons. Roofs were white and solebars were painted the body colour. Brake ends were reportedly vermilion, but it is believed that black ends became standard during the First World War.

The treatment of secondhand carriages seems to have been considerably simpler, using a 'purple brown' body paint applied at Machen. This colour was more of a reddish brown colour than on the carriages delivered new. It is believed that lining was not used, and from circa 1909 when the original B&M carriages went through shops, they were henceforth painted unlined red-brown. Some vehicles, including the saloons (which probably saw little use) remained in an increasingly shabby original lined livery. It is alleged that large class figures were used on doors from about 1909, but there is little or no evidence for this practice.

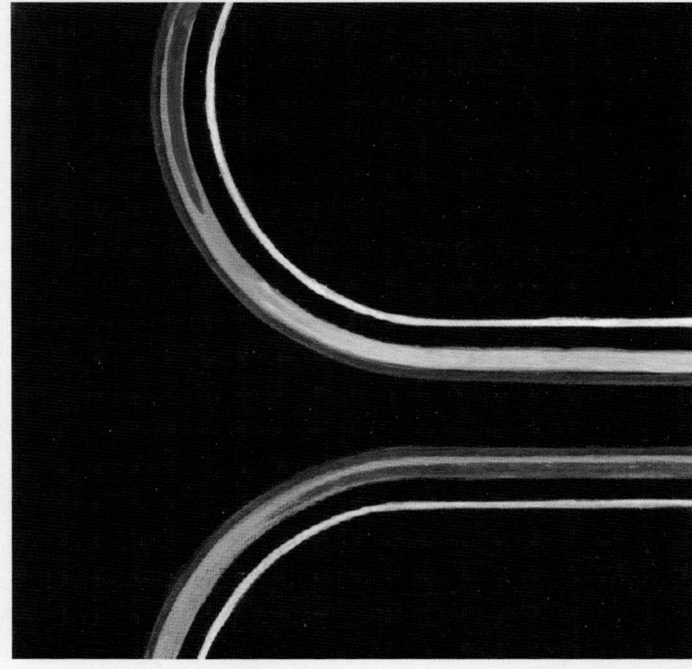

RIGHT: Original carriage lining.

Brecon & Merthyr Railway

Goods wagons were a medium grey, with black below the solebar. When new, ironwork was painted black japan, and this may have persisted in traffic, although photographs of B&M goods stock are rare. Ends of brake vans were vermilion. At first it appears there was no body lettering other than tare and load, which was in white script often shaded in black, tare being to the left. The company name and number appeared only on the solebar numberplate, which was 15 × 6 inches in size with incurved corners, with the initials "B&MR" over the number. By 1907, Machen was turning out wagons with large lettering on the sides. Where there was room, the initials "B & M" were used, the 12-inch ampersand central, flanked by 18-inch letters. On vehicles where framing intruded, for example the brake vans, only "B M" was used. The cattle wagons were lettered and numbered on the ends only, thus avoiding being obscured by the layers of limewash used to disinfect livestock vehicles.

Wagon sheets are reported in 1896 to have "BRECON & MERTHYR" along the middle, with the initials and number in each corner.

1	2	3
'Venetian Red' Carter 37 Pantone 181 BS 381 445 'Venetian Red'	'Vermilion' Carter 36 Pantone 485 BS 5252 04 E 55 or BS 381 536 'Poppy Red'	'Purple Brown' Carter 43 Pantone 4975 BS 381 541 'Maroon'

Cambrian Railways

In 1864, four small interlinked railways amalgamated to form the Cambrian Railways, followed by a fifth in 1865, resulting in a main line crossing central Wales from the Cardigan Bay coast through Newtown and Oswestry to Whitchurch on the London & North Western Railway near Crewe. The Mid-Wales Railway linked the Cambrian with the industrial railways of the south, and was worked by the Cambrian from 1888 and absorbed in 1904. In 1895 an extension to Wrexham was opened. The Cambrian was the largest Welsh railway company, yet its headquarters were in England at Oswestry in Shropshire and its traffic was largely rural. The Cambrian also worked several small standard and narrow gauge railways. Total mileage worked on all gauges in 1922 was 295 miles. The Cambrian became a constituent of the Great Western Railway in 1923 and passed into the Western Region of British Railways at Nationalisation in 1948.

Mr William Aston became Locomotive Superintendent in 1882. Until his time, all locomotives were named and the only sign of ownership was a narrow brass plate fixed on the footplate valances carrying "CAMBRIAN RAILWAY Nº xx" with the appropriate number.

Cambrian locomotives under Mr Aston were black. It has been commented that the black had a slight greenish cast to it, but (unlike the Hull & Barnsley Railway) it was not a special painting mix, and may well have been the result of many layers of varnish. Equally, it may just have been in the observer's imagination. When I did the painting in 1999, I did impart a slight greenish cast to the engine, which today I think it is best to ignore.

Lining consisted of a narrow blue-grey band flanked on each side by vermilion lines of equal width. On boiler bands there was a gap between them through which the black showed. Mr Aston abandoned the use of names and they were eventually all removed, although a few tank engines kept theirs for some time. New engines were not fitted with the old brass strip numberplate, numbers at first appearing only on the bufferbeams in gold sans-serif characters shaded in black e.g. "Nº [hook] 10". Bufferbeams were unlined vermilion [1]. Valances, steps and wheel centres, tyres and spokes were lined in vermilion. From circa 1886 the armorial device was applied on tender engines, usually on the driving wheel splasher. During the 1890s the grey lining band was broadened, with vermilion fine-lining on each side.

The armorial device consisted of a shield divided *per pale*, the dexter side charged with a Welsh dragon *en passant* and the sinister with a red rose of England. This was mounted on a trefoil, blue on locomotives, black on carriages, and surrounded by a circlet carrying "MDCCCLXIV CAMBRIAN RAILWAYS COMPANY". The Roman numerals denote the year 1864.

Elliptical brass numberplates were first used in 1888 to replace the plates carried by the engines of the Mid-Wales Railway. A

Cambrian Railways No. 36 *Plasfynnon*, built in 1863, poses with a 4-wheeled carriage and brake van circa 1900. The engine is in a transitional state, with the post-1899 livery but retaining its name. It was withdrawn in 1906. *Neil Parkhouse collection*

Cambrian Railways

standard plate was introduced in 1893, being 17 × 11 inches with "CAMBRIAN" above and "RAILWAYS" below the central number. A new lettering style was introduced in 1898, described below.

Mr Herbert Jones replaced Mr Aston in 1899. Cambrian engines were still painted black, but the grey lining was replaced by a ¾-inch yellow band, again fine-lined with vermilion. Details below the footplate were also lined in vermilion as before. Bufferbeams were now edged with black and lined with yellow, buffer casings being black. Guard irons were black, even when fitted to vermilion bufferbeams, although in some cases that part of the guard iron level with the beam was painted vermilion. Bufferbeam numbers were white, shaded in yellow and black. The inner faces of the main frames and motion parts were light grey.

Driving wheel splashers of tender engines carried the device, and tenders and tanksides now had the three feathers emblem of the Prince of Wales. This was placed centrally with the name of the company on either side in the form "CAMBRIAN [feathers] RAILWAYS". Lettering was 3½ inches high, in gold sans-serif characters, shaded to right and below in dark red, light red and white. Tender engines generally retained their cabside numberplates, but tank engines had them removed to make way for the new lettering and 6-inch brass numerals substituted on the bunker. These numerals were also used for new construction and rebuilds at Oswestry. Brasswork in the form of cleading between smokebox and boiler or safety valve seatings was kept polished. The lettering transfers supplied after about 1909 had blue shading rather than red.

From 1915, lining returned to grey. This time it was called 'French' grey, apparently slightly pinkish (again probably merely the effect of varnish), fine-lined with vermilion. Vermilion lining below the footplate was reduced or abandoned. Tenders and tanks now carried the single word "CAMBRIAN" in 7-inch unshaded sans-serif letters, in yellow and later in grey. Bufferbeam numbers followed suit, shaded as before. The device still appeared on driving wheel splashers where there was room.

Cambrian Railways

Locomotive styling after 1915.

32
Cambrian Railways

By 1883 the standard Cambrian carriage livery was 'bronze green' [2] on lower panels, upper body beading and carriage ends. The colour was simply a brownish green and should not be confused with the metallic 'bronzing' mentioned in the chapter on painting methods. Waist and upper panels were white, appearing cream under varnish. According to the *Locomotive Magazine*, lining was in gold, with black edging. This, as described rather clumsily in *Great Western Way*, was achieved by painting a black band around all mouldings, and then applying a line of unspecified width (but possibly as much as ½ inch) of gold leaf up the centre of the black.

At first there was no company lettering, only the device appearing on the lower panels. There was one centrally on short 4-wheeled carriages, and two on longer 6-wheeled and bogie vehicles. Wording in the waist was restricted to class marking in the door panels and the numbers, two on each side. Characters were gold sans-serif shaded in dark blue, light blue and white. Brake ends were vermilion, although carriages featuring end windows, such as saloons, had green lower panels and white upper panels there too.

In 1899 Mr Jones made the livery more decorative by including a thin (probably ⅛ inch) vermilion line. One source states that the previous gold lining now had a 'central' vermilion line, another states that the lining was simply yellow, fine-lined on each side with red (vermilion). The *Locomotive Magazine* notes that a single vermilion line was placed between the gold and the black. This has the ring of authenticity, being a standard method employed by the Midland Railway amongst others. The difference to modellers is probably academic, as the lines are so fine that they would be invisible in the smaller scales.

Lettering remained in the the same style and colouring, except that "CAMBRIAN RAILWAYS" in 3½-inch letters now appeared in the eaves panels, shortened to "CAMN RLYS" where space was restricted. On some carriages, where ventilators precluded eaves lettering, it was applied to the waist panels instead. The name sometimes appeared twice on the longer bogie stock. Bogie vehicles and the best 6-wheeled stock for through working now carried the feathers emblem on the lower panels, usually one centrally, with two devices either side under the waist numbers, but there were variations. Window frames and droplights were varnished wood. Roofs were white when new, and solebars were black, some apparently lined in vermilion.

From 1909 carriages were painted green only. Lining became merely a yellow line, but still applied around all mouldings. Brake

ends continued in vermilion until 1911, and from 1915 all carriage ends were painted black, again excepting those with end windows, which remained green. From the same time, roofs were painted grey, and the lettering transfers were now supplied with red shading instead of blue, without highlights.

Non-passenger carriage stock was painted the standard green, a slight difference in colour being observed, probably due to fewer layers of varnish. Lining was present, but in limited amounts. Lettering was in the carriage style, and featured the feathers emblem in gold, shaded like the lettering. After 1915, lettering on horseboxes was reduced to "CAMBRIAN" with the number below.

As far as is known, Cambrian goods wagons were always grey. Open and other general wagons were a light medium grey, including solebars, with black strapping and ironwork, and black below the solebar. Covered wagons, including vans, cattle wagons and brake vans, were a light grey with the outer faces of the outside framing painted black. Solebars on these wagons were also black.

RIGHT: Carriage lining.

34
Cambrian Railways

In the early period there was little or no lettering, except the number painted on the ends of wagons, high up in the roof quadrant in the case of covered wagons. An elliptical cast iron plate on the solebar carried "CAMBRIAN" above and "RAILWAY" below the central number until 1890, thereafter the correct plural "RAILWAYS" was used. From 1899 general stock also carried a representation of the feathers emblem centrally and a contraction of the name in the form "CAM [feathers] RYS" in white seriffed characters. Normal size was 12 inches, although it was reduced on smaller wagons, and increased to 19½ inches on the 15 ton coal wagons. It seems the early examples of this new style had the load painted in small characters on the bottom rail under the feathers, with tare on the solebar, but the standard was to have tare to the left and load to the right of the bottom rail. Body numbers were painted on the ends only, although one 1902 batch of low-sided wagons had it put below the central feathers.

Roofed wagons had the name in full, with the number centrally, for example "CAMBRIAN Nº 951 RAILWAYS" in 4-inch white characters. The new flush-sided brake vans of 1902 had "CAM [feathers] RYS" on the lower side in larger 16½-inch letters, with the number centrally above. Until about 1908 all brake vans had their ends painted vermilion.

From 1915, wagons passing through shops were painted "CAMBRIAN" in the seriffed lettering, including brake vans, and it seems a uniform grey was used for all wagons. Some wagons had a small "RAILWAYS" to one side, reputedly to distinguish them from wagons belonging to the Cambrian Colliery.

Wagon sheets originally had "CAMBRIAN RAILWAY" on each long side with the number below, but by the 1890s this was superceded by "CAMBRIAN + RAILWAYS" in seriffed lettering with the number below, and the feathers emblem to the left of the number. The cross between the words was in red and blue.

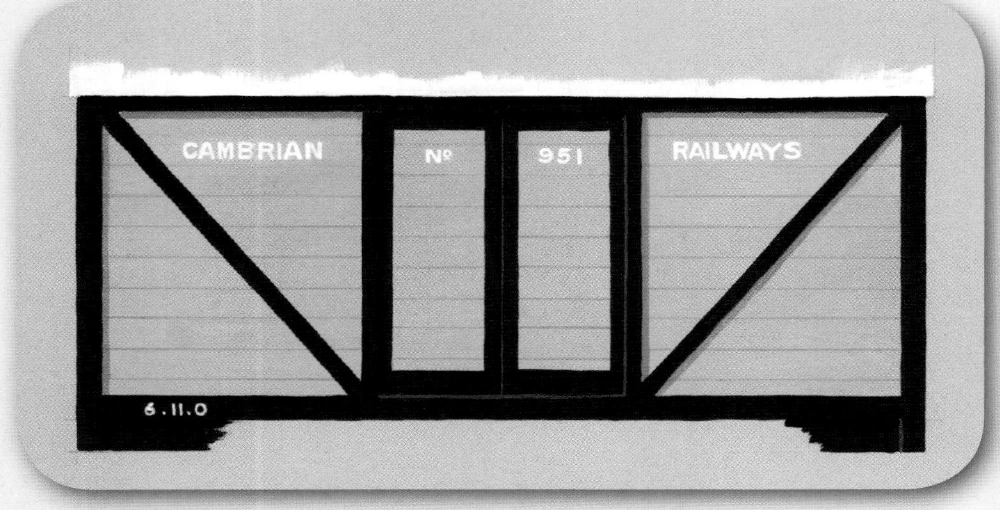

Goods van painting.

1
'Vermilion'
Carter 36
Pantone 485
BS 5252 04 E 55
or BS 381 536
'Poppy Red'

2
'Bronze green'
Carter 4
Pantone 5747
BS 381 223
'Middle Bronze Green'
or BS 4800 12 C 39
'Orchard'

Great Western Railway (1882-1904)

The Great Western was the largest pre-Grouping railway in terms of mileage and has always taken a forward position in the affections of railway enthusiasts. However, in comparison with many other railways it carried a smaller proportion of goods and mineral traffic, on a mile-for mile basis, and nearly half its length was made up of single track branches.

The Great Western was incorporated in 1835 for a broad gauge railway 118 miles long between London and Bristol. The engineer was Mr I.K. Brunel and the original lines contained many engineering innovations, not least the gauge of 7ft 0¼in. The Bristol line was opened throughout in 1841 and by association with other railways the broad gauge pushed westwards to Cornwall and South Wales, and northwards to Birmingham. However, the GW was also associating with and absorbing standard gauge railways, particularly the West Midland Railway and the railways around Shrewsbury. This, coupled with the ruling of the Gauge Commission in 1846, meant that most future lines would be mixed gauge or standard gauge only. The last line to be built in broad gauge was the St. Ives branch in 1877. Mixed gauge reached Paddington in 1861, and was extended over most of the broad gauge system. Actual conversion to standard gauge began with the South Wales line in 1872, and the last unmixed broad gauge (Exeter to Truro) was finally 'narrowed' in May 1892, after which no broad gauge trains ran.

By absorption of its associated smaller lines, the GWR expanded into a vast empire, but its axis was the London to Bristol route, which gave rise to the popular nickname 'Great Way Round'. Competition with the London & South Western Railway was fierce, but it was left until the early 20th century to improve routes with cut-offs and new lines. The length of railway maintained in 1908 amounted to 2,950 miles.

The locomotive superintendents of the GWR are a list of very famous names, but only William Dean (1877-1902) and George Churchward (1902-22) concern us here. The railway had two major locomotive centres, Swindon and Wolverhampton, and until 1894 Wolverhampton, the works of the former West Midland Railway, had its own ideas regarding liveries. From 1904 Mr Churchward instituted changes which would modernise the appearance of the railway.

The liveries of the GWR have been covered extensively in the railway press and by the HMRS, but they are still a contentious

This GWR prototype locomotive, No. 171 *Albion*, has an interesting history which allows this postcard picture to be dated to between October 1904 when it was converted to 4-4-2 and March 1907 when it was renamed *The Pirate*.

issue many decades after the organisation ceased to exist. It does not help that the references in *Britain's Railway Liveries* have been muddled, so when Carter refers to paint patch 20 as being the earlier dark green, and patch 19 as the later lighter green, he in fact means the other way round throughout. As a further red herring, the prolific railway modelling author and artist E.W. Twining insisted on specifying lighter colours; patches 20 and 15 respectively. This is only to be expected, as small models and artist's renderings *must* be painted in lighter versions, as explained in the introduction, and these would no doubt be the shades he was accustomed to using.

The locomotive livery that was current in 1890 was developed from a scheme started in circa 1882. The main colour was a dark chrome green [1]. Boiler bands and panels of lining on cabs and tenders were in black, fine-lined orange chrome [2]. Smokeboxes and chimneys were black, as were tops of splashers and footplates. Domes and safety valves were usually polished brass, and chimney caps were polished copper. Below the footplate, but also on splashers, a red-brown colour was used. Terms such as 'Indian red' and 'purple brown' are quoted, but refer to the same dark red-brown colour [3]. These areas were edged in black, and fine-lined in orange chrome. Wheels were the same red-brown with black tyres. Bufferbeams and between the frames were vermilion [4], called 'China red' at Swindon. Bufferbeams were edged in black and lined in orange chrome.

Numbers were placed on the cabs of tender engines, or centrally on the sides of tank engines, using the well-known GWR rectangular numberplate with rounded corners. A device was applied to some narrow-gauge tender engines, and an ornate intertwined script "GWR" appeared on tenders where there was room, in gold shaded in burnt sienna.

Meanwhile at Wolverhampton, locomotives were turned out in a much bluer dark chrome green, lined in black and fine-lined white. The lower parts were a darker purple brown, edged in black and fine-lined vemilion. Bufferbeams are believed to have been edged in black, fine-lined white. Other details were generally similar to Swindon practice.

In 1894 Wolverhampton officially adopted the Swindon standards,

although their blue-green persisted for several years afterwards on older engines. At the same time the base colour for all GWR locomotives was lightened slightly to a 'middle' chrome green [5], although it was still a dark colour. The first occurrence of the latter detail was on the new 4-2-2 No. 3031 *Achilles*. The lighter green was at first applied only to passenger engines, but soon became standard for all locomotives.

The bogie singles were also the subject of further elaboration. Their boiler bands were painted in a new style: green with black edges, each side of the black being fine-lined in orange chrome. This '1894 variant' was extended to a number of other express locomotives, but did not become standard throughout the stock. The 1897 Diamond Jubilee inspired another elaboration on two singles. This involved painting another orange chrome fine-line on each side of the main body lining. This '1897 variant' double lining was extended to only a handful of other engines, principally early 'Atbara' 4-4-0s. It was not a general style and had gone by 1904. There is certainly no justification whatsoever in painting the preserved *City of Truro* in this style.

Finally, from 1900 boiler bands were painted with a narrow black central portion and orange fine-lining at each edge, leaving a band of green between the two. This became the GWR standard, although the other body lining remained the same until Mr Chuchward's changes.

The device or 'garter crest' consisted of the arms of London and Bristol side-by-side within an elliptical garter, carrying the words "GREAT+WESTERN+RAILWAY+COMPANY." This was applied to the driving wheel splashers of passenger tender engines if springs did not prevent it. A number of locomotives in the 1894-95 period, principally singles, were fitted with cast versions, and small casts of the crests of London and Bristol on each side. There were also some exceptions to the rectangular brass numberplates, several 2-4-0 classes having curved numberplates, and the '3206' and '3232' classes having brass numerals set in a curve. Names became regularly used from 1893, although the nameplates were different from the later post-1904 standard. In 1899-1900, the 4-4-0s of the 'Atbara' and 'Camel' classes were fitted with large, elliptical cabside combined name and numberplates in a variety of forms.

38
Great Western Railway (1882-1904)

Carriages were painted in a two-colour livery. Lower body panels, waist panels and ends were brown, and upper panels were white, appearing cream under varnish. Droplights and bolection mouldings were varnished mahogany or painted Venetian red. Shaped wooden bonnet-type ventilators were cream, with the louvres emphasised in brown. Beading was painted black, with ¼-inch gold lining. A ⅛-inch brown line was painted around the perimeters of the cream panels, half an inch inside the beading. Roofs were white, with the rainstrip painted brown. Clerestories were usually brown, but on special vehicles (for example Royal Train carriages) were given cream panelling. Solebars were originally brown, but by circa 1900 were black, as were bogies and other ironwork.

The carriage brown was a cool middle brown, sometimes referred to as a light umber brown, and therefore possibly raw umber. Unfortunately, no specification has survived. The 'cream' was officially referred to as white. The cream effect was probably the result of several coats of varnish, but remains would tend to indicate that the white was actually an off-white to start with, although this may just be the effect of age on the white lead pigment. From 1903 the colours were changed to become much richer, dealt with in the next chapter.

Lettering in the waist was in gold seriffed characters, shaded black, and was usually confined to class marking on each door. Numbers were placed in the eaves, also in gold and black but sans-serif. Most stock carried two numbers placed as symmetrically as possible, but long bogie stock had three. On the lower panels were a variety of embellishments. Throughout this period, Thirds, Seconds and Brake vehicles usually had two small "GWR" entwined script monograms. Until circa 1900, Firsts and Composites had two of the gartered devices placed symmetrically; on short vehicles this usually meant on the two middle doors. After that date, just one device was placed centrally, but the two small crests were placed along the carriage on either side – London to the left, and Bristol to the right.

Non-passenger stock was painted coach brown all over, and lettered in yellow. Lettering was small, and on horseboxes shaded in black.

Great Western Railway (1882-1904)

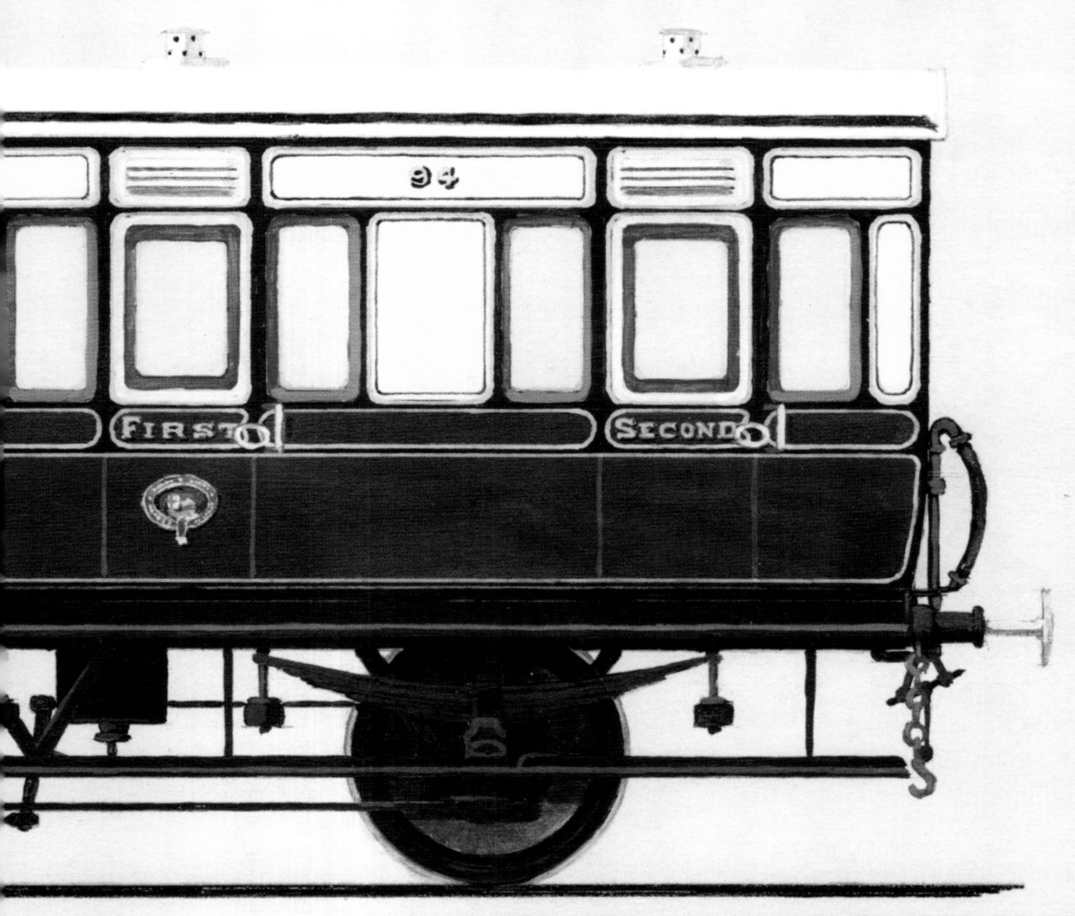

Postcard view of GWR 4-4-0 No. 3433 *City of Bath* with a rake of clerestory carriages, posted in 1904.

Great Western Railway (1882-1904)

Wagon painting is the subject of controversy. Wagons were originally painted in 'light red', the lightest member of the iron oxide series. It is known that from the 1880s goods brake vans were painted dark grey and it is believed that grey may have begun to be applied to other stock too. However, the bulk of the general wagon stock remained in the original light red until at least 1896 and, if contemporary observers are to be believed, considerably later than that. The uniformly grey method of painting was almost certainly established at the time of Mr Churchward's changes in 1904.

Lettering on wagons was in small white characters "G.W.R" with full stops. Originally the initials were on the lower left, with number on the lower right. Permissable load was painted in script lettering above or below the initials, and tare was associated with the number. From 1893 the respective positions were switched, so that initials were on the right, possibly coinciding with the application of grey as each wagon was painted. There were no numberplates at this time, but wagons had the initials and number painted onto the solebar.

Wagon sheets had the initials "G W R" on all four sides. Below the main side lettering was the number and the manufacturing date, and at each end numbers were placed diagonally in each corner so that they were visible when the sheet was mounted on a wagon. At the centre was a short white bar across the main axis, with a small "GWR" above and the number below. Above the initials at each end was a simplified dragon's wing. After 1903 the initials used were "GW" and the wings were omitted.

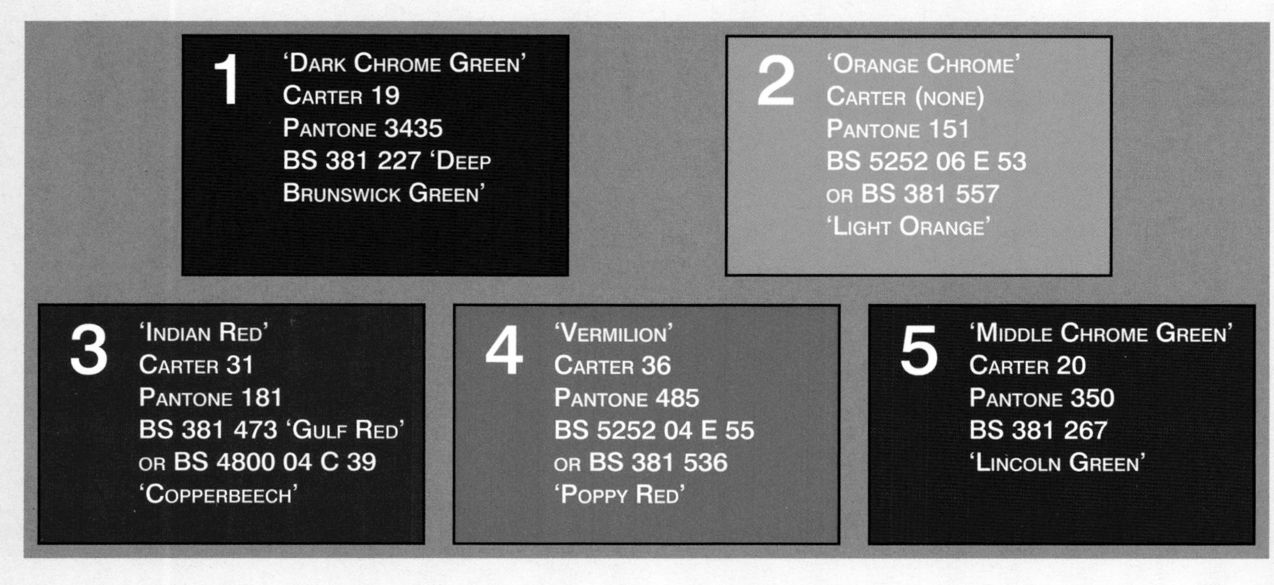

Great Western Railway (1905-1922)

As the GWR moved into the 20th century several cut-off lines were built, the principal one being between Castle Cary and Langport (1906) which shortened the route to the West of England by twenty miles. The same year saw the opening of the joint line with the Great Central Railway, followed by the 'New Line' via Bicester to Birmingham in 1910. At Swindon, Mr Dean retired and a new hand took the helm, that of George Jackson Churchward (1902-22). The Great Western was the only former company to take its name unchanged into the Grouping of 1923. The new company had a virtual monopoly in the west and south-west of Great Britain and preserved many of the practices of the old company right through the Grouping era and after Nationalisation in 1948, when it became the Western Region of British Railways.

Great Western locomotives in 1902 were painted a middle chrome green, and wheels, splashers, valancing and outside frames were purple brown, as denoted in the previous chapter. Mr Churchward had been appointed as Works Manager at Swindon in 1896 and became Mr Dean's Chief Assistant in 1897. His presence soon made itself felt, culminating in the building in 1902 of No. 100, the prototype outside-cylinder 4-6-0 on the GWR, later named *William Dean*. Contemporary coloured illustrations of this engine reveal the anachronistic appearance of the old livery on such a large locomotive. A second prototype 4-6-0, No. 98, came out of Swindon in 1903 with Mr Churchward's new coned boiler – and brown below the footplate but with green splashers. The writing was on the wall for the Dean livery and the last new construction to carry it appeared in early 1905, for example 4-4-2 No. 179 *Magnet*.

The new Churchward livery was much simpler. The middle chrome green [1] was retained, but everything below the footplate was now black, lined sparingly with orange chrome [2], outside cylinders with a double line. The standard boiler band lining was extended to the rest of the body, there being half an inch of green showing between the middle black band and the orange chrome outer lining. Tenders were lined in one panel and carried the lettering "GREAT [device] WESTERN" in gold seriffed characters shaded in vermilion. The device at this time was similar to the old one, with the arms of London and Bristol side by side within a garter, but it was less elliptical than the older design. Copper chimney caps, brass safety valve bonnets and other beading remained polished. Cab roofs, footplates, smokeboxes and so on were black.

A postcard view of GWR 4-4-0 No. 4107 *Cineraria*. Built in 1908, it was fitted with a superheater in November 1911 and renumbered as 4155 in December 1912.

Great Western Railway (1905-1922)

Great Western Railway (1905-1922)

Great Western Railway (1905-1922)

The numberplates of new tank engines were positioned on the bunkers, but the change to existing stock was not rapid; many remained on tanksides for several years. At first the lettering was "GREAT WESTERN" without the device, but by 1907 the device was being used routinely.

Bufferbeams were vermilion [3], edged with black and orange chrome. From 1900 the engine numbers were being applied in transfers in yellow, shaded black, in the usual form, for example "N° [hook] 3202". By 1910 only the number was being used. Numberplates were brass with a black ground to the polished seriffed numbers. A thin orange chrome line was painted around the perimeter of the black. From 1902 names were carried on plates curved over the splasher tops of passenger engines, in polished seriffed letters on a black background, the combined name and number plates for the 1898-1901 'Camels' and 'Atbaras' being abandoned. The curved plates were at first taken completely around the splasher, the well-known segmental design not appearing until 1904.

During the First World War many locomotives emerged from the paint shop unlined and with metalwork painted over. There were also difficulties obtaining paint and the shades of green varied considerably. After the war, henceforth only the express engines were fully lined, tank engines and goods engines remaining unlined with no polished metal. This was the style that took the GWR into the Grouping era.

Carriages in 1902 were painted in the style evolved many years previously, as denoted in the previous chapter. The first hint of change came in 1903. During that year, the standard colours were altered to a darker, redder brown [4] and a deep cream [5]. As the *Railway Magazine* put it: 'The new tints have certainly a warmer and richer appearance than the original colours'. The same magazine also reported an experimental painting of one rake of coaches in an 'all-chocolate colour'. This experiment must have been successful, because from September 1908 the livery that had served the GWR since the 1860s was abandoned.

RIGHT: GWR 'Saint' Class 4-6-0 No. 2902 *Lady of the Lake* hauled the first GWR two-hour Birmingham to Paddington train in July 1910. The postcard credits this picture as being the 'Birmingham and North Express (via the new route) near Acton.'

Great Western Railway (1905-1922)

46

Great Western Railway (1905-1922)

Carriages were now painted the darker brown [4] all over, except for the carriage ends, which were black. Beading was no longer black although the lining was as before, apparently in yellow ochre paint at first, but from 1910 restored to gold leaf. Roofs were white and underframes were black, although wheel centres were 'red oxide'. The lettering was also modernised. The new characters were seriffed gold as before, but now shaded in red and white to stand out more against the dark brown. The initials "GWR" were placed on the waist panels, two to a side in a symmetrical arrangement. Beneath the left-hand initials was placed the small dragon's wing crest of London, with the crossed arms of Bristol below the right-hand set. The device was placed centrally on the lower panels. Class marking was still in words on the doors. Numbers were in smaller sans-serif numerals, placed in the waist at each end of the vehicle.

The change to brown was not generally liked, the *Railway Year Book* for 1909 bemoaning that the colouring was 'changed from the popular tea-brown and cream to red-chocolate brown'. Worse was to come, for in 1912 the carriage colour was changed to crimson lake [6], very similar to the Midland Railway colour. On the crimson scheme, the initials "GWR" appeared once centrally, with

the device below. Other details were the same, except that droplights and window mouldings were now painted the body colour, instead of venetian red or mahogany. The white roofs had a 2-inch black border at each end. An interesting detail was the polishing of the brass door hinges.

Finally, in July 1922 a start was made at restoring the pre-1908 colours, complete with black beading lined with gold. Even smooth steel-sided stock was panelled out by the painters as if it had beading, and lined accordingly, this habit starting in the crimson period when steel coaches first appeared. One difference was that the fine inner lining on the cream panels was omitted. Ends were black. Lettering positions remained unchanged from the crimson period, although the shading reverted to plain black. Droplights and window mouldings were 'mahogany colour'. This style survived until 1927, when conventional lining was abandoned altogether.

Non-passenger vehicles such as horseboxes were painted carriage brown, changing to crimson lake in 1912 and reverting to brown in 1922. Lettering was always in yellow, small at first but from 1903 in the large initials "G W" up to 25 inches in height. In common with goods stock, smaller 16-inch initials were adopted in 1920.

Great Western Railway (1905-1922)

Wagons in 1902 were probably a mixture of dark grey and light red vehicles. The lettering was in 6-inch white characters, with numbers on the left-hand side of the body and "G . W . R" on the right. Numbers were also painted on the ends of wagons. From the mid-1890s, small rectangular cast iron plates were used for this lettering on new stock, with the characters picked out in white.

In 1904 the appearance of ordinary goods stock was standardised by the universal application of dark grey. Van roofs were white, and refrigerated and insulated vehicles were painted white with lettering in red. The dark grey is reported as being based on three coats. The first two were lead white 'mixed with a little black', and the top coat of black 'mixed with a little lead white'. Unfortunately quantities are not specified, but I would suggest that a lot more of the additive colour than is implied by 'a little' was required.

At the same time the initials "G W" were introduced on all wagons. These were as large as possible, up to a maximum of 25 inches. Numbers maintained the GW tradition of being painted on the left below the "G". Below the "W" were painted the permissible load and tare in italic script. A rectangular solebar plate carrying "G.W." over the number was also introduced. The large letters persisted until 1920, when a smaller 16-inch size was adopted as standard, which was used until 1937.

1 'Middle Chrome Green' Carter 20 Pantone 350 BS 381 267 'Lincoln Green'	**2** 'Orange Chrome' Carter (none) Pantone 151 BS 5252 06 E 53 or BS 381 557 'Light Orange'	**3** 'Vermilion' Carter 36 Pantone 485 BS 5252 04 E 55 or BS 381 536 'Poppy Red'
4 'Carriage Brown' Carter 46 Pantone 4625 BS 4800 08 B 29 'Vandyke Brown' or BS 381 413 'Nut Brown'	**5** 'Carriage Cream' Carter 45 Pantone 7508 BS 5252 08 C 33 or BS381 386 'Champagne'	**6** 'Carriage Crimson Lake' Carter 28 Pantone 188 BS 381 540 'Crimson'

Mersey Railway

There were several schemes proposed in the mid-nineteenth century to connect the Wirral peninsula with Liverpool across the River Mersey using bridges or tunnels. The Mersey Railway itself was inaugurated in 1866 as the Mersey Pneumatic Railway, engineered by Sir Charles Fox and supported by the MPs for Liverpool and Birkenhead, as a single line of railway in a tube under the river. Air power to suck and blow the trains was proposed. A second Act was obtained in 1868 which changed the name to Mersey Railway. The rather eccentric pneumatic method of locomotion was abandoned in an Act of 1871 and alteration made to allow a double line. A contract for construction was signed in 1872 and work started, but the contractor John Dickson got into financial difficulties. For the next nine years all attempts to raise more capital and resume work failed. Finally, at an Extraordinary General Meeting in 1881, a new Board was elected and new shares issued; this enabled construction to begin in earnest.

The double line tunnel was steeply graded to dive beneath the river and was accompanied by two smaller tunnels, one for drainage and the other for ventilation, which was achieved by steam pumping engines and large fans on each shore. The initial section of the Mersey Railway between Green Lane (Birkenhead) and James Street (Liverpool) was opened for traffic on 1st February 1886. The line attracted an average of 6 million passengers per annum, but this was not enough and at the end of 1887 the Mersey was put into receivership. It was seen as important to complete the planned extensions in order to save the railway. The branch to meet the Wirral Railway (as it would soon become) at the joint Birkenhead Park station was opened on 2nd January 1888, the extension to the joint Great Western/London & North Western line at Rock Ferry in June 1891, and Liverpool Central, beneath the Cheshire Lines station, was opened in January 1892. Despite proposals for various goods lines, this was the furthest extent of the Mersey Railway, 4¾ miles.

Early locomotive livery for the Mersey Railway.

The passenger numbers declined through the 1890s due to the atmosphere in the tunnel, made unpleasant by the steam locomotives, despite the use of condensing equipment and the best efforts of the ventilating system. The Corporation tramways also made deep inroads into the revenue when they were electrified in 1901. Electrification had first been proposed in 1895 and further powers were obtained in 1900, but nothing was done by the Board, which by this time was in severe disarray. Salvation came in that year from the British Westinghouse Electric & Manufacturing Co. Ltd, who were looking for a line to electrify in order to demonstrate their equipment. The Mersey seemed ideal, and the contract was signed in 1901. Work proceeded rapidly and the last steam train ran on the 2nd May 1903. Financial recovery of the railway was steady thereafter. The Mersey Railway remained independent of the Grouping in 1923, but was absorbed into the London Midland Region of British Railways in 1948. It still serves the public as part of the Merseyrail system.

To cope with the severe gradients, the locomotives supplied by Beyer, Peacock were small but very powerful tank engines, fitted with condensing equipment and cabless, having only spectacle plates to protect the enginemen. The first nine were 0-6-4Ts built in 1885 with double frames, as illustrated. The next six were 2-6-2Ts, the first of this wheel arrangement in Britain, built in 1887; they had conventional inside frames, with radial trucks at front and rear. The final three 2-6-2T locomotives were not supplied until 1892, and were built by Kitson. They were very similar to the Peacock engines except they had rather unattractive extended smokeboxes of smaller diameter. All engines were named, the nameplates being fixed to the boilers. Numberplates were fixed to the centre of the side tanks.

The livery details of the Mersey Railway are sparse and no drawing of a wagon could be found, so the painting shows a locomotive and a carriage in the livery they are believed to have carried at the time of electrification. There were few references in the railway press, the most comprehensive being the livery notes in *The Locomotive Magazine* Volume 2 (1897) and Volume 8 (1903).

The main locomotive colour was described as medium green, which was used on boilers, tanks, bunkers, sandboxes above the footplate and wheels. On the flat surfaces, the medium green was edged by a darker green. Further decoration changed over time, the original lining being more ornate than that used later. In this livery there was a vermilion line between the approximately 4 inches wide dark green edging and the mid-green body colour. About 3 inches within this edging was a 2 inches wide band of lining in black,

50
Mersey Railway

fine-lined on the outer edge with vermilion and on the inner edge with white. On the sandboxes above the footplate, space was limited and so the dark green edge abutted directly onto the lining. Boiler bands were black, lined with vermilion, and wheel tyres and axle ends were also black, lined in vermilion. Smokeboxes, chimneys, condenser pipes and tank venting chimneys were black. Both sets of chimneys were copper-capped.

Everything below the footplate other than wheels was brown, including frames, valances, steps and outside cylinders, probably the 'purple brown' favoured by many railways of the time. Edging was in black, fine-lined in vermilion. Bufferbeams were also vermilion, edged in black, with the number appearing in the usual form, for example "N^{O} [hook] 12", in gold seriffed characters shaded in black. Outside cranks were vermilion.

The rectangular nameplates were in brass with seriffed characters on a vermilion background. Numberplates were elliptical brass, with a large central seriffed numeral and "MERSEY RAILWAY" in small letters over it. Underneath was the date of construction. The background was again vermilion.

This original livery survived on some locomotives into the 20th

century, but from 1892 and the delivery of the Kitson 2-6-2Ts the livery style adopted a simpler form. The body colours remained the same, but the black lining was now fine-lined in white only. The dark green edging was expanded to about 6 inches wide and the vermilion line abandoned, the main lining now acting as the boundary between the two colours. Treatment of the purple brown areas remained the same. The new livery was gradually applied to the rest of the locomotive stock, but it seems that not all had been so treated by 1903.

Although most engines had their names and numbers removed and were sold after electrification, steam did not entirely disappear. Mersey No. 4 *Gladstone* was retained until 1908 for service use until being replaced by an ex-Metropolitan 4-4-0T (No. 61), which became Mersey No. 1. This was in turn replaced by Mersey No. 2, another ex-Met 4-4-0T (No. 7) in 1925, and again in 1939 by Mersey No. 3, an ex-Great Eastern 0-6-0T. Livery details are virtually non-existent, but it is possible that all three were painted black. Lettering on the first two seems to have been "MERSEY" with the number beneath, but the third engine was simply lettered "M E R", again with the number below.

52
Mersey Railway

Carriage stock in the steam era consisted of ninety-seven vehicles, all 4-wheeled, arranged in sets of eight with brake vehicles at each end. As built by the Ashbury Company, the carriages were varnished teak, but the harsh conditions in the tunnel seem to have forced the railway into painting them a medium brown colour, in imitation of the original varnished wood. Lining around the panels was in yellow, fine-lined vermilion. Brake ends were vermilion and a photograph shows lining on the beading here too. Solebars and underframes were black. Roofs were white, no doubt rapidly changing to sooty black.

Carriage lettering is difficult to determine. There was no company name in the waist panels, the only sign of ownership being the garter device. This simply carried the title "MERSEY RAILWAY COMPANY" in gilt, and inside was a representation of the Liver

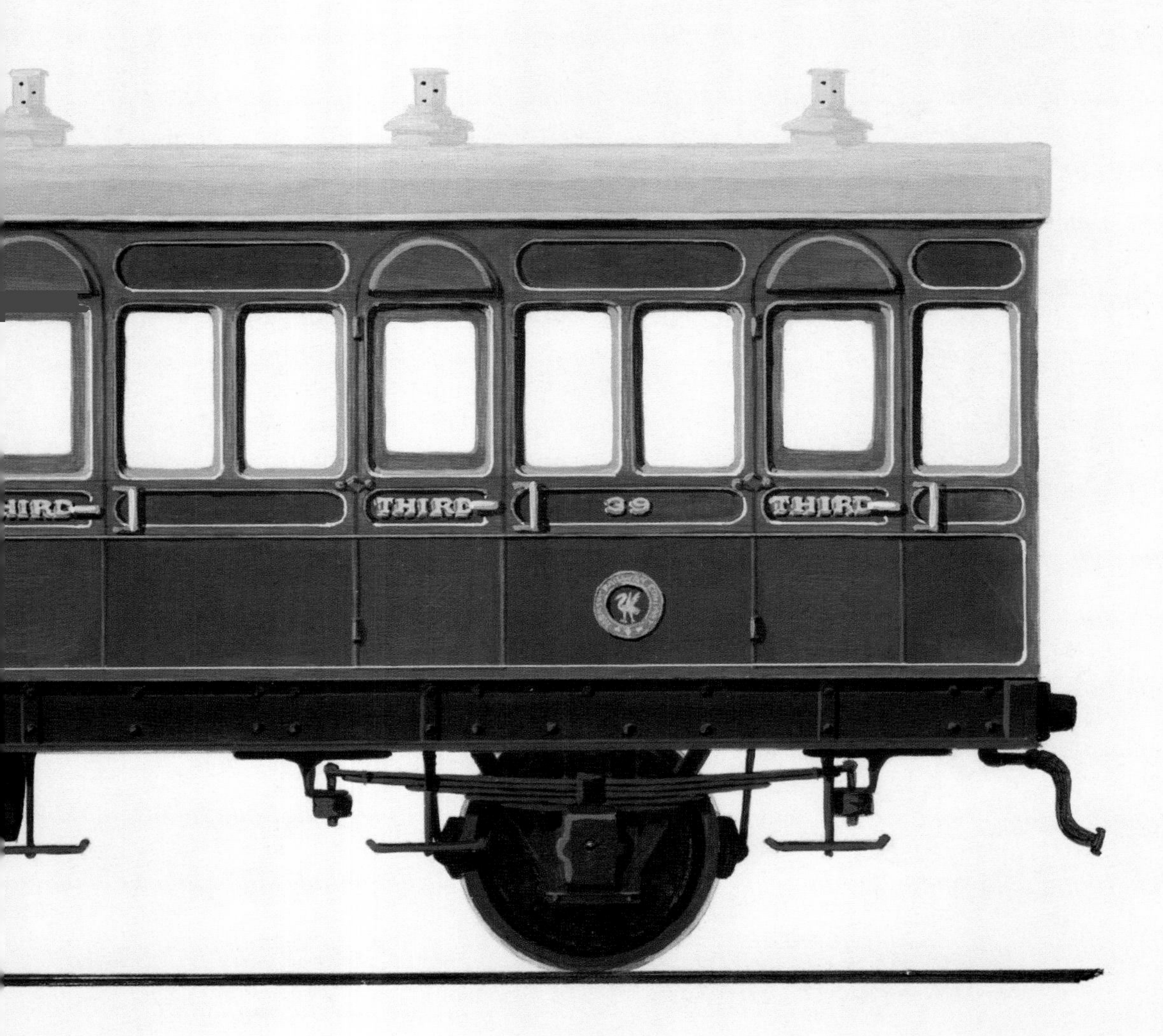

bird. The device seems to have been used twice on each side, with the vehicle number above it in the waist. It seems that originally class marking was in words in the waist panels of the doors, for example "THIRD". The brake compartments had "GUARD" on one door. Characters were in yellow and it looks like a seriffed style was used. Shading was to left and below in white and 'chocolate', probably a crimson colour, shadowed in black. However, by the time of electrification, large seriffed class numerals were being applied to the lower door panels of stock and the class wording was abandoned. This is very much in line with the style later adopted for the electric stock.

As a passenger railway, goods stock was not really necessary except for service use. The Mersey possessed one goods brake van, one goods wagon and four ballast wagons. They were painted dark grey with white lettering. The style of this lettering is unknown.

Mersey Railway No. 6 *Fox*, built by Beyer, Peacock & Co. for the opening of the line in 1886, carrying the original style of lining.
John Alsop collection

Mersey Railway No. 12 *Bouverie*, built by Beyer, Peacock & Co. in 1887, in original livery, with a set of Mersey 4-wheeled carriages glimpsed behind.
John Alsop collection

Midland & South Western Junction Railway

A direct line connecting Southampton with the industrial Midlands was first proposed in the 1840s, but it was not until 1872 that a more modest scheme of joining the Great Western at Swindon with the London & South Western at Andover was promoted. The Swindon, Marlborough & Andover Railway was opened in stages in 1881 and 1882. The nominally independent Swindon & Cheltenham Extension Railway was formed in 1880 to take the line northwards to Cheltenham, opening to Cirencester in 1883 and Andoversford Junction near Cheltenham in 1891. The Midland & South Western Junction had been created from the amalgamation of the two companies in 1884.

Through-running of M&SWJ trains to Southampton began in 1892 and through carriages were operated by the Midland Railway from as far afield as Sheffield. The avoidance of a short stretch of GWR between Savernake and Marlborough was achieved by the opening of the Marlborough & Grafton Railway in 1898. This line was double track, but the rest of the railway was single until 1900-1902, when more of it was doubled. Length, including a short branch from Ludgershall to Tidworth military camp, was 64½ miles. The railway's locomotive, carriage and wagon workshops were at Cirencester.

The M&SWJ became a constituent of the Great Western Railway in 1923, and passed into the Western Region of British Railways at Nationalisation in 1948.

The SM&A locomotives, all with side tanks, were painted in a very similar style to that of the GWR at the time: dark green, presumably with red-brown frames and wheels. Lettering was sans-serif in gold, shaded in blue, in the form "S.M.& A.R^{Y} N^{O} [number]" with full stops. Domes were polished brass and chimney caps were polished copper. Lining generally had incurved corners.

By about 1890, the M&SWJ had adopted the Midland manner of locomotive painting, using the same 'crimson lake', or alizarin crimson [1]. Panels were edged in black with yellow fine-lining, and lining and boiler bands were also black edged on both sides by yellow, just as on the Midland. Wheels were crimson with tyres, edges of wheel bosses and axle ends all black, lined with yellow. It also seems that frames were crimson in the earlier period, edged with black and yellow, but by 1914 frames appear to be black, with only guard irons and other items such as sand boxes and bogie compensating beams in lined crimson. Bufferbeams were vermilion [2] edged in black, lined white.

Some sources report that 'goods locomotives' were 'olive' green, but it appears that the only engine to be painted this way was 2-6-0 No. 14 of 1895. Its sister engine No. 16 of 1896 was in lined crimson.

The first standard lettering was "M.& S.W.J.R^{Y} N^{O} [number]" on the tanksides, in gold sans-serif characters shaded in blue and shadowed in black, with prominent full stops. The first tender locomotive, 4-4-0 No. 9 of 1893, had just the initials "M.& S.W.J.R^{Y}" on the tender, and a small elliptical brass numberplate on the cab with a vermilion background. The 2-4-0 and 0-6-0T locomotives delivered in 1894 had the same.

In 1895, full stops and numberplates were abandoned, as 0-4-4T No. 15 and 2-6-0s No. 14 and No. 16 of that year can show. These engines carried brass numerals, those on No. 15 being central on its tanks with the lettering disposed on each side "M & S 15 W J R^{Y}".

Midland & South Western Junction Railway No. 11, built by Dübs & Co. of Glasgow in 1894, outside Swindon Town shed in April 1921, with the final script lettering on the tender.
Neil Parkhouse collection

The other two engines had "M&SWJR^{Y}" on the tenders. Further developments in lettering were seen on the 0-6-0 locomotives numbered 19 to 28 ordered from Beyer, Peacock, delivered in 1899 and 1902, which had a similar style with brass numerals on the cabs but the ampersand was omitted, "MSWJR^{Y}" appearing closely-spaced on the tenders, still in the sans-serif characters.

Meanwhile at Cirencester, independently of the new construction mentioned above, seriffed characters similar to those on the Midland Railway became the vogue, and full stops reappeared, giving rise to a bewildering variety of lettering. Ex-SM&A locomotives were being turned out with even more full stops than formerly, for example "M. &. S. W. J. R^{Y}. N^{O} 2."

However, the two 4-4-4Ts numbered 17 and 18 of 1897 were delivered from Sharp, Stewart & Co. carrying only "M.S.W.J.R" in seriffed characters. Numbers were also transfers, rather than brass numerals.

The next new engines were the 4-4-0s delivered between 1905 and 1914. All these engines had a new style brass numberplate on the cab, being rectangular with rounded corners, simply carrying the number on a vermilion background. The first example, 4-4-0 No. 1, carried "M.S.W.J.R" in seriffed characters, but on the rest of the engines the full stops were omitted, and "MSWJR" became the standard form of lettering between circa 1905 and 1913. Engines generally emerged after repainting at Cirencester with the same style of characters they carried before (serif or sans-serif), but the new simplified "MSWJR" was universal.

An exception was the 0-4-4T No. 15, which retained its ampersand, as the lettering would have been unbalanced without it. Unusually, the brass numerals were given shading to conform with the rest of the lettering.

The final change was instituted in 1913. All former lettering was replaced on engines passing through shops by a decorative "MSWJR" in entwined gold script, shaded in black. Numberplates and brass numerals were normally left as they were, but 0-4-4T No. 15 and 4-4-4T numbers 17 and 18 received large transferred numbers instead of their former brass numerals. Simultaneously with this lettering change, the 0-6-0s numbered 19 to 28 were painted black. No. 19 had some vermilion and white lining, but the rest remained unlined. On the black livery, the script monogram was yellow rather than gold.

New script locomotive lettering of 1913.

Midland & South Western Junction Railway

The SM&A 6- and 4-wheeled carriages were delivered in a dark all-over colour, probably brown, but by 1884 were reported as being painted brown and cream in very similar colours to GWR carriages. The sans-serif lettering was reported as being gold, shaded in blue. Manufacturer's drawings imply that SM&A class marking was in words, numbers were in the eaves panels and the company name appeared on a garter in the lower panels.

The two-colour approach was still in use as late as 1896, when most of the SM&A carriages were refurbished at the Gloucester Railway Carriage & Wagon Co. The lower part of the body was painted brown, with the cream applied on the waist and the upper panels. There was limited lining around some of the panels, apparently in brown. Lettering was applied in simple unshaded sans-serif characters, again probably in brown. Lettering on the 6-compartment stock was "M&SWJ^{N}R^{Y}" placed centrally, with two numbers on the waist to either side. Class marking was still in words.

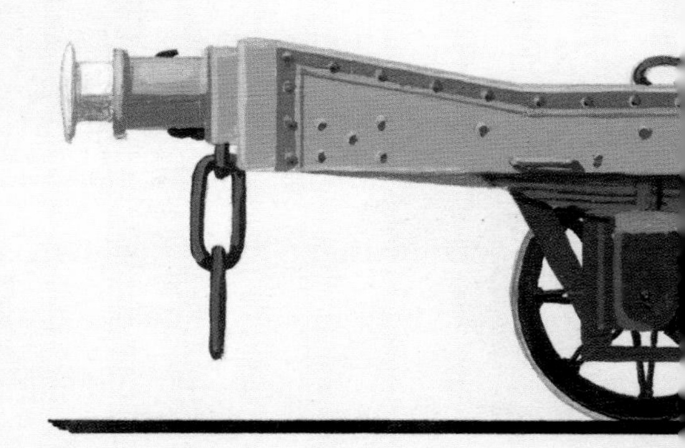

From 1893 new carriages were constructed and, apart from some L&SWR details, they were almost identical externally to Midland

COND
SECOND
25
SECOND

MSWJR
212

carriages. They were all painted in the Midland style, being crimson lake [1] with black beading, lined gold and fine-lined vermilion. It is noteworthy that between 1909 and 1917 a number of ex-Midland carriages were added to M&SWJ stock, and these were virtually indistinguishable from the home carriages.

The refurbished ex-SM&A carriages were eventually repainted in crimson, but there is some doubt regarding the lining, which was yellow rather than gold. The beading and arrangement of the body panels did not lend themselves to a conventional style as on the Midland-type carriages and it is possible that they were lined only in yellow. However, a part view of one of the carriages outside the paint shop at Cirencester implies that the upper beading was indeed painted black. Unfortunately, the lower part of the body is obscured and it is not possible to see how they handled the junction between black and crimson at the waist level.

All carriage solebars were probably crimson at first, edged in black as on the Midland, but black became the standard. Roofs had been white until the crimson livery was adopted, when they are believed to have become lead grey, another Midland practice. By 1914 carriage ends were being painted black.

Lettering on the crimson livery was "MSWJR", the number in gold sans-serif characters shaded black on the new carriages, and yellow shaded in red on the old. Class marking was still in words. Second class was abolished in 1904, but the markings would have persisted for some time.

NAYLOR'S SMOKESTACK BLACK

NAYLOR BROTHERS (London), LTD.
Varnish Specialists,
407 & 409, OXFORD ST., LONDON, W.

NAYLOR'S RELIABLE RAILWAY VARNISHES

Non-passenger coaching vehicles such as horseboxes and milk vans were probably painted coach brown in the earlier period, and then crimson. Lettering consisted of the initials "M&SWJR^{Y}" on the brown and "MSWJR" on the crimson.

Goods stock of the SM&A was painted a dark colour, either dark grey or brown. Lettering was "S.M & A.R^{Y}" on the left side with the number on the right in small white characters. There was an elliptical numberplate on the solebar.

The M&SWJR adopted a light grey body colour and it appears that numberplates were not used. All below the solebar was painted black, and when first delivered body metalwork and steel solebars were also black; this is believed to have been replaced by grey on repainting. From about 1917, the grey was described as being medium or dark grey.

Lettering was in white, and for most of the life of the company was about six inches high. By 1896 the ampersand had been omitted so that the standard form of lettering was usually "M.S.W.J.R" to the left and number to the right on both open wagons and vans. Some low-sided wagons and vans delivered in 1896 were given their initials centrally with the numbers below. The vans probably kept this arrangement as, unlike the other vans, they had a sliding door. A number of open wagons delivered in 1900 had lettering twice the size, spaced out along the whole side as "M. & S. W. J. R", but this arrangement did not persist. On manufacturer's photographs the lettering was shaded in black, and on the whole it seems this was maintained in general service. From circa 1900 the full stops were omitted.

Brake vans had differing approaches. Outside-framed vans had the initials and number on one line, for example "M S W J R 17", but those brakes with plain matchboarded sides had the initials centrally in a larger size, with numbers below.

Wagon sheets had the initials "M & S W J^{C} R^{Y}" in large block characters, with numbers below in seriffed numerals.

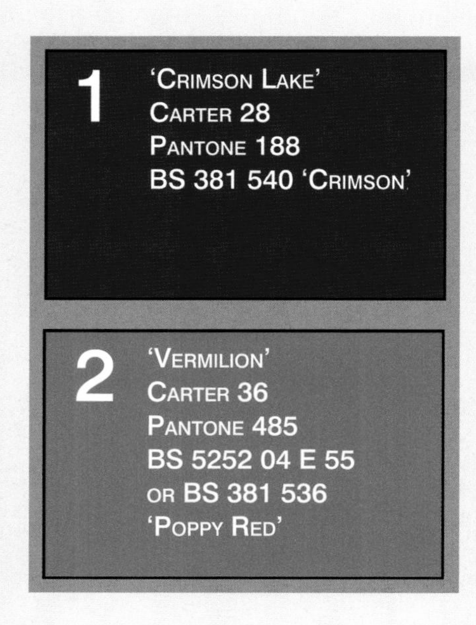

Rhondda & Swansea Bay Railway

Whilst the coalfields of South Wales had been tapped by many railways, most of the coal traffic flowed down the valleys to docks around Cardiff. The city of Swansea found this intolerable. A public meeting was held there in 1880 and the result of this meeting, the Rhondda & Swansea Bay Railway, obtained its first Act of Parliament in 1882. The intended route was easterly from Swansea, across the Neath estuary to Aberavon and Port Talbot, then north-east up the Afan Valley, partly along the route of the former Cwmavon Tramway, to tunnel under the towering Mynydd Blaenrhondda into the Rhondda Valley, joining with the Taff Vale Railway at Treherbert.

The first section along the Afan Valley was opened in 1885, followed by the 3,463 yard tunnel to Treherbert in 1890. The original plan had been to use running powers from a junction at Aberavon to work over the Great Western Railway into Swansea, but the GWR was being so obstructive that the R&SB powers granted by the first Act lapsed. Another Act had to be obtained in 1891 for an independent line into Swansea, including a new branch to Neath. Mineral trains were running from the Rhondda through to Swansea Docks by 1894 and passenger trains traversed the whole route from 1895. To facilitate through working to the TVR, the brakes on the carriages and locomotives were altered from their original Westinghouse fittings to automatic vacuum. The company's works were established at Danygraig near Swansea in 1896 and were presided over by Mr R. Oliver.

The GWR eventually became more reasonable. Friendly overtures were made, finally resulting in an offer to work the R&SB with a guarantee of an increased fixed dividend. The terms were accepted and the GWR worked the R&SB from 1st July 1906. Although there were some additions to locomotive stock and replacements of rolling stock, the line retained its own identity until absorbed by the GWR in 1922. The R&SB therefore passed into the Western Region of British Railways at Nationalisation in 1948.

Apart from two early engines, the first standard locomotives received by the R&SB were five 0-6-0Ts built by Beyer, Peacock between 1885 and 1889, and one 0-6-2T (No. 4) by Kitson & Co. in 1886. The latter engine was very similar to the TVR Class 'M' and features in the painting. The R&SB decided that this wheel arrangement was ideal for its needs, including the steep climbs up the Afan Valley, and a further twelve 0-6-2Ts of slightly larger dimensions than No. 4 were delivered by Kitson between 1889 and 1899. Two larger but similar engines built by Stephenson & Co. were purchased from the Port Talbot Railway in 1901, and finally four much enlarged 0-6-2Ts were delivered by Kitson in 1904. For passenger traffic, three 2-4-2Ts arrived from Kitson in 1895.

Locomotives were painted black, kept very glossy by the cleaning staff. Lining on tanks, bunkers and boiler bands was in blue, probably ultramarine, with slightly narrower lining on cabs, cab fronts and sandboxes. In addition, valances and steps were edged

Rhondda & Swansea Bay Railway No. 25, built by Kitson & Co. in 1904, showing how handsome a black livery could be. The blue lining is very easy to see, registered as very pale by the photographic emulsion, but the vermilion lines are more elusive although still visible on the bunker. Notice that whilst the rear of the bunker is lined, the back of the cab is not. *Author's collection*

with blue, and wheel centres had a ring of blue. A short distance away from the blue were fine-lines of vermilion, the black showing between.

Bufferbeams were vermilion [1], edged with black and lined in white. They carried the engine number in the normal way, "N^{O} [hook] 16" for example, apparently in gold seriffed letters shaded in blue, shadowed in black. The motion and inside faces of the frames were probably vermilion, as was usual at that time, and cab interiors were a pale colour, probably cream or buff.

No lettering was carried by the engines, but every one was fitted with a numberplate on the centre of the side tanks, surrounded by a fine vermilion line. The numberplate was elliptical in brass, with a wide, polished border on which the name "RHONDDA & SWANSEA BAY RAILWAY" was etched and filled with black wax. The central portion was vermilion; the *Railway Magazine* remarked in 1900 that although both the R&SB and the Taff Vale used black, the Rhondda company's engines could be easily recognised by their red numberplates. In the border below the central number was the date of construction. The Beyer, Peacock 0-6-0Ts had a slightly different design, in which the border was omitted and each number was preceded by "N^{O}". The latter engines also did not have the armorial device transferred on the centre of the bunker as applied to all the 0-6-2Ts and 2-4-2Ts, because the builders plate was placed there. The device was rather unusual in having a pictorial representation of both an engine and a ship, each in their own little circle of landscape on a dark green background, within a garter carrying the name of the company. A fine vermilion line encircled the device.

After the agreement in 1906, the GWR transferred ten of their 0-6-0Ts to R&SB stock, which were numbered into the R&SB series in order to appease the TVR at Treherbert, who pointed out that the running powers into that station only applied to the original company, not the GWR. There is evidence to suggest that the GW painted its R&SB engines plain black, without lining. Certainly, when rebuilt in 1921, 2-4-2T No. 19 was finished this way, although retaining its original numberplate.

RIGHT: Rhondda & Swansea Bay Railway No. 20, built by Kitson & Co. in October 1899, in unusually disreputable condition. *John Alsop collection*

Rhondda & Swansea Bay Railway

Rhondda & Swansea Bay Railway

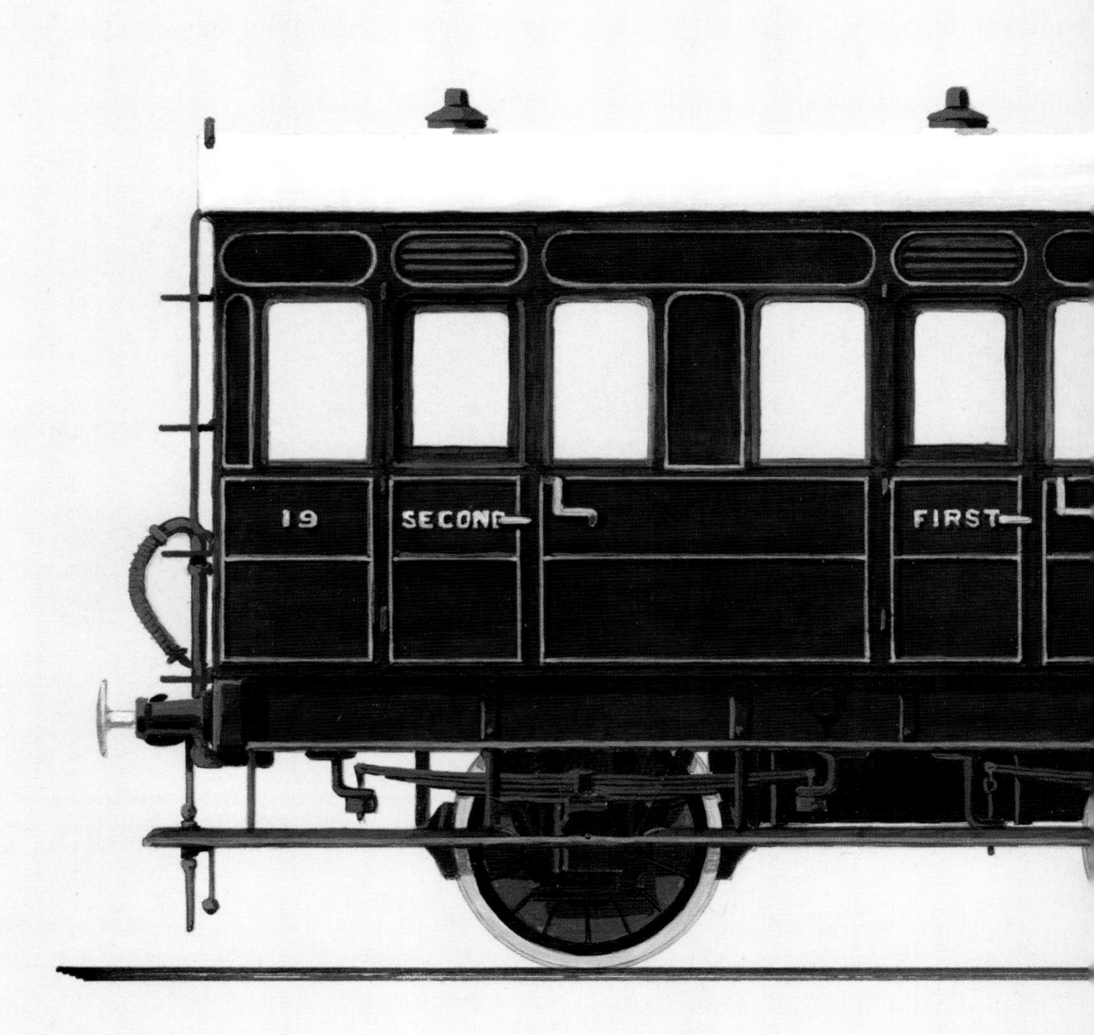

The original carriage stock of the railway was 6-wheeled, supplied by Brown, Marshall & Co. A reporter for *The Cambrian* newspaper on the opening day gives some useful data. There were three classes (First, Second and Third) and the exteriors were painted lake red, 'a tinge darker' than Midland Railway carriages [2], picked out with yellow and gold. Another source gives the body colour as 'chocolate', which is quite in accord with a carriage colour of dark crimson. Lining appears to have been in yellow.

Lettering is uncertain, since photographs are almost nonexistent, but it seems that characters were sans-serif in gold. Class marking was in words on the waist panels of the doors and the numbers were two to a side, positioned symmetrically; a photograph of Composite No. 19 waiting to be scrapped at Swindon in 1924 shows the numbers on the panels at each end. Ownership was apparently denoted by a script rendering of "R&SBR" in gold, similar to that used by the Rhymney Railway. This was placed centrally on Composites, but may have appeared twice on other stock, with the armorial device below on the lower panels.

Rhondda & Swansea Bay Railway

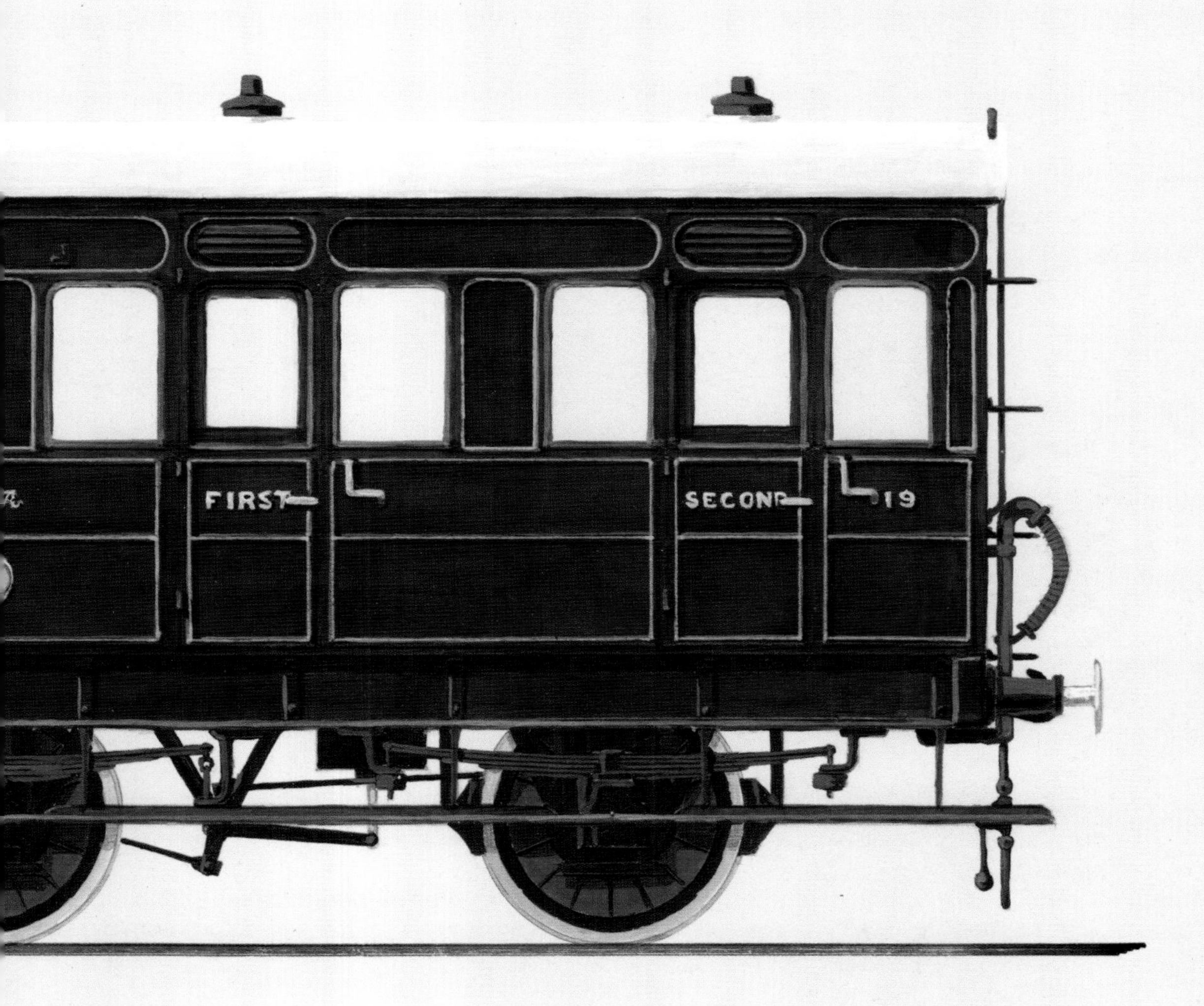

In 1895 the Ashbury Railway Carriage & Iron Company supplied twenty-six 41 foot bogie coaches for the new through services. With their clerestory roofs and red-brown colour, the railway author Hamilton Ellis observed that they had a resemblance to carriages of the North Eastern Railway.

After the GWR agreement, carriages going through the paint shop were painted in the standard GWR colours of the time, although the R&SB lettering remained in use. One casualty of the change in working company was the loss of Second Class. Composite No. 19 has boards bearing the word "THIRD" in standard GWR seriffed lettering fixed over the former Second Class markings. Ironically, the adoption of GWR colours would not have been much of a change, as it will be remembered that GW carriages were painted brown from 1908, and crimson from 1912.

There were a small number of non-passenger vehicles such as horseboxes and carriage trucks, and it is likely that they were treated in a simplified form of the passenger livery, probably unlined, with lettering in yellow.

Rhondda & Swansea Bay Railway

For the opening, a small number of wagons were supplied by the Gloucester Wagon Co. These wagons were painted 'chocolate', according to the official photograph of mineral wagon No. 38, on which "RHONDDA & SWANSEA BAY R^{Y}" was painted in white letters.

However, by 1895 wagons were being painted light grey. Lettering was simplified to "R.&.S.B.R^{Y}" in approximately 6-inch sans-serif characters, although sometimes the superscript "^{Y}" was absent. Vans and cattle trucks had the letters spaced out between doors and framing, with the loss of some of the full stops, and the number painted below on the right. Open wagons had the initials grouped together on the left-hand side, with the number in a corresponding position on the right. Loco coal wagons had these initials and number on the lower part of the side, with a larger "LOCO DEP^{T}" painted along the top.

Official photographs show black shading to the lettering, black strapping, and white wheel tyres, but it is unlikely that these were present on vehicles in traffic. Load was shown in italic script, and tare in small numerals separated by points. The R&SB do not appear to have used a numberplate on the solebars. Wagon sheets are reported as simply having the usual initials, no doubt with a number, but no other distinguishing features.

1 'Vermilion'
Carter 36
Pantone 485
BS 5252 04 E 55
or BS 381 536
'Poppy Red'

2 'Crimson Lake'
Carter 28
Pantone 188
BS 381 540 'Crimson'

Rhymney Railway

The Rhymney (pronounced 'Rumney') was an example of one of the fiercely independent coal-carrying lines of South Wales. Despite only having 51 route miles, including 10 miles of joint lines, the Rhymney paid dividends to its shareholders which were the envy of many large railways. The railway was promoted by the Marquis of Bute's trustees as a way of connecting his Cardiff Docks with the Rhymney Ironworks and coalfield. The single line was opened in 1858 from Rhymney to a junction on the Taff Vale Railway, with a branch to Caerphilly and more rails in Bute East Docks. The year 1871 was an important year, when a direct line to Cardiff from Caerphilly was opened, as was a joint line with the London & North Western Railway, giving a northern outlet. Doubling of the main line began in 1872, and the Taff Bargoed joint line with the Great Western Railway opened in 1876.

The Rhymney did have Locomotive Superintendents, Mr Richard Jenkins occupying the post from 1884, but the Traffic Manager Mr Cornelius Lundie exerted so much authority that he dominated locomotive matters until his retirement in 1904. The appointment in 1906 of Mr C.T. Hurry Riches (son of T. Hurry Riches of the TVR) introduced a period of significant change and he remained in post until the GWR absorbed the Rhymney in 1922. The Rhymney passed into the Western Region of British Railways at Nationalisation in 1948.

The Rhymney had its own locomotive and carriage works in Cardiff, and from 1902 at Caerphilly, but engines were built by outside contractors. Among the first locomotives were three inside-frame 2-4-0s built by the Vulcan Foundry, which originally carried a curved brass plate over the driving wheel splashers, combining the

Standard locomotive numberplate.

Rhymney Railway 'J' Class No. 50, built by Sharp, Stewart & Co. in 1884. The locomotive is seen at Cardiff Docks circa 1900, in original condition, fully lined out, carrying the distinctive cast RR numberplate and coupled to 4-wheeled brake van No. 26.
John Alsop collection

owner's intials with the number, for example "R R C^{O} N^{O}16". Six 0-6-0s, also from Vulcan Foundry, carried a straight brass plate on the boiler which again combined the name and number in the form "RHYMNEY [number] RAILWAY" on a black background, this becoming the standard plate for nearly all engines. Only the four 0-6-0s with outside frames from Kitson & Co. carried a special plate with the number above the name, as shown in the main illustration. In addition, all engines carried brass numerals on the chimneys and on the rear of bunkers or tenders. Some engines had polished brass domes. From 1872 until 1904, the dominant type of locomotive on the Rhymney was the outside-framed 0-6-0 saddletank.

Locomotive body colour was a dark Brunswick green [1]. Panels such as cab sides, bunkers and saddletanks were edged with black, separated from the green by a thin white line. Body lining was black, fine-lined with white on each edge, the corners of the lining being incurved. Saddletanks were lined out in two panels, the standard numberplate being placed centrally on the lower edges of the tanks, over the junction between the two. Boiler bands were black, fine-lined on each side with white. Bufferbeams were vermilion, edged with black and white.

Below the footplate, both inside and outside frames were red-brown, termed 'chocolate', bordered with black and fine-lined white. Wheels were green, with black tyres edged with white. Wheel centres and axle ends, where visible, were also lined in black, fine-lined in white. It seems most coupling rods and outside cranks were vermilion [2], although the ends of the rods, the bushes and oiling cups were left polished metal.

The device, consisting of the arms of Cardiff and Newport within a circular blue border bearing the company name, was employed on bunker sides (space permitting) by 1896.

From 1904 all new engines were ordered (from R. Stephenson, Hudswell, Clarke and Beyer, Peacock) with conventional side tanks. For the first of the new breed, the six Class 'M' 0-6-2Ts, colour and lining remained as before, but they were fitted with a small elliptical brass numberplate bearing "RHYMNEY" above the central number and "RAILWAY" below on a black background, placed at the centre of the side tanks. The device was on the bunker, chimney numbers were omitted.

From 1909, brass plates were abandoned altogether on new construction and all old numberplates were removed. Lining on

Locomotive lettering after 1909.

Rhymney Railway 'J' Class No. 52, was built by Sharp, Stewart & Co. in 1884 but is seen here after rebuilding with a larger, more modern cab in 1905. It carries the later style of unlined green and black livery and has lost its numberplate in favour of the new gold letters and numbers.
John Alsop collection

Rhymney Railway No. 64 was originally built as a 2-4-2ST in 1890, rebuilt by the Rhymney Railway as an 'L1' Class 0-6-2ST in 1911. The engine is in plain green and black with the later lettering. The number on the rear of the bunker is noteworthy.
John Alsop collection

Rhymney Railway 'K' Class No. 85, built by Sharp, Stewart & Co. in 1897, in the later plain livery reserved for older engines.
John Alsop collection

Rhymney Railway 'R' Class No. 44, at Cardiff Docks in 1921, the year of its construction, displays the simplified lined livery applied from 1909 to the newer engines. The lining has conventional corners, the lettering transfers are gilt shaded in light green, and the bunker bears the new circular device.
John Alsop collection

the recent classes (almost entirely 0-6-2Ts) was simplified to have conventional rounded corners, but the saddletanks and surviving older engines were no longer lined at all and were turned out in plain green, with black below the footplate. Locomotives were now lettered in a new standard, having "R [number] R" in gold characters, shaded in light green to the right and below. The initials were approximately 9 inches high, with the numbers in a smaller size of approximately 6 inches. During the 1914-18 war, some locomotives were reportedly painted black.

From 1882 the Rhymney began building its own 6-wheeled carriages. Others were obtained from the usual rolling stock suppliers and also secondhand. Bogie stock began appearing from 1900. The lower parts of carriages were described as 'chocolate', 'maroon' or 'purple brown' [3], a dark red-brown, with upper panels in 'cream', which was white under varnish. The *Railway Magazine* remarked in 1900 that 'the carriages somewhat resemble those of the LNWR'. Early 4-wheeled vehicles had all above the waist in white, apparently picked out with fine purple-brown lining, but the 6-wheeled vehicles introduced a new standard of purple brown waist panels and upper beading, leaving only the upper and eaves panels in white. Lining was a single yellow line around the beading. Droplight frames were varnished mahogany, roofs were white, and carriage ends were black.

Carriage lettering was gold, shaded to right and below in red. The layout was generally a symmetrical arrangement of two numbers between the outer compartments at each end, with devices below, and two ornate monograms of "*RR*" in interlaced script letters on the next panels within. Class marking was in words on the door waist panels. From 1907, carriages began to be painted purple brown all over, lined in yellow, and possibly fine-lined in red. Lettering was simplified to "R R" in block characters. Class marking was now in large seriffed numerals on the lower part of the doors.

RIGHT: Four-wheel First/Second Composite No. 64 illustrates the older stock of the Rhymney Railway. Under the coal dust it can just be seen that the 'white' of the upper body is applied to all features, including the waist panels and beading. The placing of a device below each number was standard Rhymney practice. *John Alsop collection*

Rhymney Railway

Although *Moore's Monthly Magazine* (later *The Locomotive Magazine*) in 1897 states that good stock was painted dark red, it is generally accepted that wagons were painted a dark grey, very similar to that of the GWR. Wooden solebars were also grey, although steel solebars were black, as was everything below the solebar. The *Railway Clearing House Handbook* of 1896 notes the use of "RHYMNEY" in full on wagons, however it seems lettering was generally "R R" about 12 inches high, placed centrally on each portion of the side and also appearing on the ends. Loco coal wagons had the initials at the top of the sides with "LOCO [door] COAL" below. Covered vans and goods brakes had the initials in the upper corners of each side. Numbers were at bottom left, prefixed with "N°".

Between 1904 and 1912 wagon lettering increased in size to about 24 inches high, positioned immediately on each side of open wagon doors, or on the doors of vans. The prefix was dropped from wagon numbers. Loco coal wagons now had small lettering "LOCO COAL" on the lower plank of the side door. As far as is known, goods brake vans always had their ends painted vermilion.

Later wagon lettering.

1	2	3
'Dark Brunswick Green'	'Vermilion'	'Carriage Purple Brown'
Carter 9	Carter 36	Carter 29
Pantone 350	Pantone 485	Pantone 483
BS 381 226	BS 5252 04 E 55 or BS 381 536	BS 381 448
'Mid Brunswick Green'	'Poppy Red'	'Deep Indian Red'

Taff Vale Railway

The Taff Vale was one of the oldest railways in Wales, having been incorporated in 1836. A certain Mr Brunel laid out a route between Merthyr Tydfil and Cardiff Docks. The original line was opened throughout in 1841, but by construction of branches and absorption of other local railways, the TVR came to own several lines penetrating the valleys northward and westward. The Penarth Harbour, Dock & Railway scheme, opened in 1865 and leased by the TVR, extended its dock facilities. The total mileage was 124, traversed by a great many coal trains: goods and mineral train mileage in 1908 was 1,672,834 miles. This ensured receipts were healthy and the TVR was one of the best-paying British railways.

The Taff Vale became a constituent of the Great Western Railway group in 1923 and passed into the Western Region of British Railways at Nationalisation in 1948.

The early livery of TVR locomotives was dark green, with venetian red or 'chocolate' frames, and until 1862 they carried names rather than numbers. Under Locomotive, Carriage & Wagon Superintendent Mr Tom Hurry Riches (1873-1911) engines were painted a red-brown colour, lined with black edged with vermilion [1]. Locomotives had chimneys finished with a brass cap, and those few engines considered as 'passenger' had polished brass domes and safety valve seatings.

While the red-brown was retained for the passenger engines, the 1880 batch of 0-6-0 goods engines introduced black to the railway and most new construction was henceforth painted black. Mr Hurry Riches introduced the Class 'M' 0-6-2Ts in 1885, the first of a long line of similar engines. These were painted black, including domes and safety valve seats, but still had brass chimney caps. It is clear from early photographs of this and other classes that the main lining, while disposed in three lines on panels in a similar way to that used later, at this stage consisted of two vermilion lines with a yellow one between them. Frames, wheel cranks and splashers were lined with two lines of vermilion and yellow only, the vermilion being outermost. Boiler bands had a central line of yellow, edged on each side with vermilion.

Tank sides carried an elliptical brass numberplate featuring a broad outer border with the number in relief in the middle, apparently on a red background. The words "TAFF VALE" were etched in the border above the number and "RAILWAY" below. The plate was outlined in yellow.

Taff Vale Railway No. 32 was built as an 0-6-0 tender engine by the Avonside Engine Co. in 1871 and converted to an 0-6-0ST in 1886. Ilt is seen here circa 1890, in black, but with the earlier lining and first style of numberplate. *John Alsop collection*

The device featured a Welsh dragon holding a shield, surrounded by a garter carrying the words "TAFF VALE RAILWAY COMPANY" and the date 1836. Surmounting the garter was a mountain goat crest and the motto "Cymru a fu Cymru a fydd". Until about 1900 the garter was an elliptical shape, but then became circular. The normal position was on the bunkers of tank engines but in the earlier black period it could also be seen on the boilers of 0-6-0s.

From the introduction of the Class 'O' 0-6-2Ts in 1894, the livery changed slightly. Chimneys were no longer brass capped and a more conventional elliptical brass numberplate with narrow border appeared. The number was central on a red background as before. Over the number was "TAFF VALE RAILWAY" in small letters and below was the date of construction. Locomotives built at West Yard Works also had "CARDIFF WORKS" and, where rebuilding work had taken place, the word "REBUILT" inserted immediately below the number. Several engines received new plates in exchange for their old ones.

Perhaps the most noticeable development was the adoption of an inner white line for the triple lining of the larger body panels, replacing what had formerly been vermilion. This appeared on sides and fronts of tanks, sides and rear of bunkers, and often on cab sidesheets, but where space was limited the white line could be omitted. Lining on cab fronts, cab rears, valances, sandboxes and axle ends remained the usual vermilion and yellow. Wheel tyres were lined in vermilion. Vermilion also appeared on safety valve levers and springs, and apparently on coupling rods, which had formerly been kept polished.

Bufferbeams were subject to some variation. Originally they were

panelled to each side and between the buffers with black and yellow, with "N^{O} [hook] 33", for example, in gold characters, shaded in black. Buffer casings were vermilion, the outer lip and buffer seat being black, separated from the vermilion by a yellow line. By 1912, and also by some outside builders before that, bufferbeams were being painted more simply, with just a black border and yellow line. Buffer casings were vermilion with only the outer lip painted black, lined yellow.

The passenger locomotives began appearing in black in the early 1890s, and by 1900 had assumed the standard black livery, although they retained brass fittings until the 1914-18 war or when rebuilt.

Mr Hurry Riches was a devotee of steam railcars, and sixteen were in service. The engine part was painted black and lined out in a similar way to the other locomotives – the red, yellow and white lines following the rather boxlike shape. The earliest examples had a numberplate incorporating "N^{O}" before the number, but later ones had the standard numberplate.

Mr Hurry Riches was succeeded by his assistant Mr J. Cameron in 1911. Mr Cameron produced the Class 'A' 0-6-2Ts from 1914. These were painted unlined black and had a new rectangular design of numberplate, but no device. The engines produced in 1921 once more carried the device on the bunker, but for some reason the garter resumed its earlier elliptical form. Bufferbeams were plain unlined vermilion.

The painting depicts a Class 'N' 0-6-2T locomotive of 1891. The rather odd lining on the cab side is caused by a sliding panel, used to cover the cab cutout, being pushed nearly fully open.

Taff Vale Railway No. 91 was built for the Metropolitan Railway in 1868 and was one of four of sold to the TVR in 1873-74. It is seen here as rebuilt in 1884, carrying the black livery with earlier lining and first numberplate. This engine was withdrawn in 1898. *John Alsop collection*

Taff Vale Railway 4-4-0T No. 68 was one of a class of three engines built at the TVR's Cardiff West Yard Works 1884-85. Although it still has the first numberplate, the engine is lined in the new standard red/yellow/white combination. Note how the painters have omitted the inner white line on the restricted areas of the bunker and sandbox. *John Alsop collection*

Taff Vale Railway 'C' Class No. 171, built by the Vulcan Foundry in 1888, carries the later lining scheme but has retained its polished brass chimney cap, a feature abandoned on later engines.
John Alsop collection

A beautifully clear view of the lining of a Taff Vale Railway engine in the standard period. The second type of numberplate and the new circular device are also apparent. TVR 'U' Class No. 194 was another Vulcan Foundry product, built in 1895.
John Alsop collection

Taff Vale Railway

Carriages were painted brown and white. Lower panels, carriage ends and solebars were specified as 'purple brown to pattern' [2] with three coats of hard drying varnish. Panels from the waist upward were painted white, then finished with 'varnish colour' (in other words a typical enamel coat) and three coats of varnish. This gave a pale 'primrose' aspect to the white, which darkened over time. The purple brown was extended up into the white area as a band around the mouldings. The actual lining was in yellow, with a thin line of vermilion between the yellow and purple brown. Ventilators were purple brown with each louvre lined.

Below the solebar was black, as were buffers, steps and handrails on the carriage ends. Roofs were white, including lamps and other fitments. Wheels were the Mansell type, with varnished wood centres and white tyres. Droplights were varnished mahogany.

Lettering was in gold, shaded to the left in yellow and below in vermilion and maroon, and shadowed in black. The waist panels of doors carried class marking in words, but company identity was restricted to the device, which was applied to the lower panels – usually two per side arranged symmetrically, the carriage number appearing in the waist panels above each. The carriage portions of steam railmotors had their class marking in the form "FIRST CLASS" and "THIRD CLASS". There were three devices on each side of most examples and the number was painted on the solebar.

It is believed workmen's trains and certain other carriages during the 1914-18 war were painted purple brown all over, with "TAFF VALE RAILWAY" and the number in plain yellow characters in the waist. Non-passenger stock was also painted purple brown; a photograph of a meat van shows small lettering "T.V.R", possibly in yellow, shaded in the same way as on passenger stock.

In a specification of 1873, wagons were to be painted light grey. However, by 1898 and probably much earlier, wagon colour was brown oxide [3]. Roofs were white and body ironwork was black, at least when new. To the left-hand side, on the lowest plank of open wagons or about the fourth plank up on vans, were the letters "T.V.R." in white six-inch block letters with square full stops. In

a corresponding position to the right-hand side was the number. Builders' photographs often show the white lettering shaded in black, but this is unlikely to have been applied in service. On the bottom rail under the initials was the tare in italic characters. Brake vans, which had their ends painted vermilion, had the initials centrally, about halfway up the body side. Below was a plate carrying the name of the guard and often the allocated working.

From 1903, numberplates were introduced and numbers painted on the body generally abandoned. Solebar numberplates were elliptical, with "TAFF VALE" over the number and "RAILWAY" under. Letters and border were white on a black background. Wagon ends featured small plates carrying the number only, also in white on black. Initials were still to the left, with tare below on vans, or to the right on open wagons, now in small block characters.

RIGHT: Carriage upper body lining.

The final change occurred in 1909, when the small lettering was superceded by the large letters "T V", about 16 inches high. The large initials were positioned high up on the body and usually towards the ends. Tare was again generally on the right. Body ironwork was now also brown oxide, black being used below the solebar.

Wagon sheets were lettered "T.V.R.943" (for example) on each side and end, and featured a cross made up of one red line painted from corner to corner, crossed by a green line painted between the other corners.

Earlier small wagon lettering.

1 'Vermilion'
Carter 36
Pantone 485
BS 5252 04 E 55
or BS 381 536
'Poppy Red'

2 'Carriage Brown'
Carter 39
Pantone 4625
BS 5252 06 C 40

3 'Brown Oxide'
Carter 30
Pantone 4695
BS 381 490
'Beech Brown'

Wirral Railway

Few railways of so small a size, 13½ miles, could have had such a complicated history as the Wirral Railway. The WR carried a heavy passenger traffic, serving the northern residential districts of the Wirral peninsula, connecting with Liverpool via the Mersey Railway and the ferry at Seacombe. However, this residential development did not get into its stride until the latter part of the 19th century, and the early history of the railways that were to become the WR was one of financial difficulty.

The Hoylake Railway was opened from Birkenhead to Hoylake in 1866, but was put up for sale and working suspended as the result of a Chancery Decree in 1869. In 1872 its assets were acquired by the Hoylake & Birkenhead Rail & Tramway Co. and reopened. The Act allowed the construction of a street tramway to Woodside Ferry and an extension of the line westwards to West Kirby, opened in 1878. The tramway was transferred to Birkenhead Corporation Tramways in 1879. In 1881 the company changed its name to the Seacombe, Hoylake & Deeside Railway and obtained authorisation to extend to Seacombe and New Brighton.

The name 'Wirral Railway' first appeared in 1883 as a nominally separate company to build a line down the centre of the peninsula from Bidston to join the Wrexham, Mold & Connah's Quay and Manchester, Sheffield & Lincolnshire railways, and also to extend eastwards in Birkenhead to join the Mersey Railway, then under construction, at a new joint station, Birkenhead Park. The latter was effected in 1888, but the former ambition had encountered difficulties and was made over jointly to the WM&CQ and MS&L in 1889 and opened by them in 1896. This line became entirely Great Central in 1905.

Finally, the Wirral Railway proper was incorporated in 1891 to buy the shares of the SH&D and Wirral (1883) railways and merge them into one undertaking. Apart from the doubling of the main line and provision of new workshops at Birkenhead Docks, there was little further development. It was planned to electrify the Wirral to coincide with the electrification of the Mersey Railway in 1903, but finances would not allow it.

The Wirral Railway was included in the London, Midland & Scottish Railway group in 1923, and the LM&S carried out the electrification in 1938, except on the Seacombe Branch. Through running of the new three-car electric sets over the Mersey Railway into Liverpool commenced immediately. Both lines passed into the London Midland Region of British Railways in 1948 and now form part of the Merseyrail system.

The liveries of the WR have never been adequately studied and much more work needs to be done. This chapter presents the information as currently understood.

The original Hoylake Railway possessed two locomotives, both secondhand and both obscure. It is not until the reopening in 1872 and the appointment of Mr J.E. Medley as Locomotive Superintendent that more information is forthcoming. Two secondhand engines were purchased, ex-L&SWR 2-2-2WT *Comet* in 1872 and an ex-Neath & Brecon 2-4-0WT in 1879. Both apparently retained the liveries in which they arrived. It has been suggested that the L&SWR engine was green, but L&SWR locomotives were brown at the time.

In 1877 two new 2-4-0T locomotives arrived from the Yorkshire Engine Co., No. 1 *West Kirby* and No. 2 *Birkenhead*. All subsequent new engines were purchased from Beyer, Peacock of Manchester. Under the name of the Seacombe, Hoylake & Deeside Railway, two more 2-4-0Ts were ordered (numbers 3 and 4), followed by five 0-4-4Ts (numbers 5 to 9). The livery was at first described as

Brake Composite No. 76 was a one-off built for the Wirral Railway by the Brush Electrical Engineering Co. in 1906 specially for the Seacombe–New Brighton service. This photograph clearly shows the lined crimson of the carriage livery and the typical layout of the lettering. The only signs of company ownership are the two devices. *Neil Parkhouse collection*

'chocolate', lined in black and vermilion. The expression 'chocolate' is frustratingly inexact, and had a different meaning from our present day usage for Victorian commentators. For example, Midland Railway engines were often described as being 'chocolate', meaning a deep, rich crimson. Thus SH&D engines could have been the browner shade of ex-L&SWR *Comet* or Midland crimson.

It is alleged that the SH&D adopted a black livery during its tenure. However, looking at the 'works grey' photographs taken by Beyer, Peacock, and bearing in mind that it is unwise to place too much reliance on them as indicators of true livery, I would suggest that the earlier livery was still in use when 0-4-4T No. 6 was delivered in 1887. The only indicator of ownership was on the tankside numberplates, which were elliptical in form with an outer rim and a border area delineated by a second raised rim inside it. The number was on the central portion, for example "N^{O} 6", with the initials "S H & D R^{Y} C^{O}" in the upper part of the border and the date of construction in the lower part. Raised figures and border were polished brass, and the background vermilion. Apparently by 1891 a black livery had indeed been adopted, which differed only from the Wirral livery described below in the design of the numberplates.

Locomotives continued to be built by Beyer, Peacock; from 1892 according to the specifications of Mr E.G. Barker, and from 1902 Mr T.B. Hunter, but they had little to do with the detail design of the locomotives. Numbers were carried on from the SH&D list. The first Wirral engine was a 4-4-2T (No. 1), followed by two more 0-4-4Ts (numbers 7 and 10). In 1896 a 4-4-4T (No. 11) arrived, honoured as the first of this wheel arrangement in the British Isles. Two more 4-4-4Ts of a larger size arrived in 1903. The two large 0-6-4Ts (numbers 12 and 13) meant to handle the increasing goods

85
Wirral Railway

traffic had arrived in 1900. The last new engine for the WR was yet another 0-4-4T (No. 3) in 1914.

The livery of Wirral engines was black. Bufferbeams were vermilion [1] edged in black, fine-lined white. Buffer casings were black and the number appeared in gold seriffed characters shaded in black, for example "N^O [hook] 12". Locomotive lining was in two forms. Firstly, a thin vermilion line followed the edges of cabs, valances and steps, appeared around the ends of bufferbeams, which were black, and on the inner edge of wheel tyres. There may also have been a circle of lining on wheel centres. Boiler bands were edged in vermilion. Secondly, tanks and bunkers were lined boldly into panels with a broad white band. About 2 inches inside these panels was another thin vermilion line.

On the cab side sheets was the device. This was a garter carrying the word "WIRRAL RAILWAY" surrounding a hunting horn 'proper' suspended from a decorated lanyard. The tankside numberplates were elliptical with raised rim, carrying the number centrally and "WIRRAL RAILWAY C^O" over it. Below was the date of construction. Coupling rods were vermilion, although there are reports of some being 'lake' (that is, crimson) edged with black and vermilion. Cab interiors were vermilion or green, the former probably the standard Beyer, Peacock finish.

There were no changes in the livery, except that the device seems to have been omitted from about 1909 when engines were reboilered. Even when four ex-L&NWR 2-4-2T and an ex-L&Y 2-4-2T were purchased secondhand in the years 1913-21, the standard Wirral livery was applied, without device. The only differences appeared on numbers 16 and 17, which featured painted numbers, as no Wirral cast plates were available for re-use. These numbers may have been gold or yellow.

Wirral Railway

The early carriages are virtually unknown, although Mr Medley acquired some Neath & Brecon Railway stock. However, from 1888 new carriages were purchased and when the Wirral Railway was formed there were forty-three passenger vehicles, increasing to eighty-four by 1908. Between 1910 and 1914, several bogie coaches were formed by combining two old 4-wheeled bodies on a new underframe.

Carriage livery was described as 'dark lake' or a 'rich chocolate shade'. This is likely to be very similar to the Midland Railway carriage crimson [2]. Lining was in yellow around the mouldings, fine-lined with vermilion. Lettering in the waist panels was limited

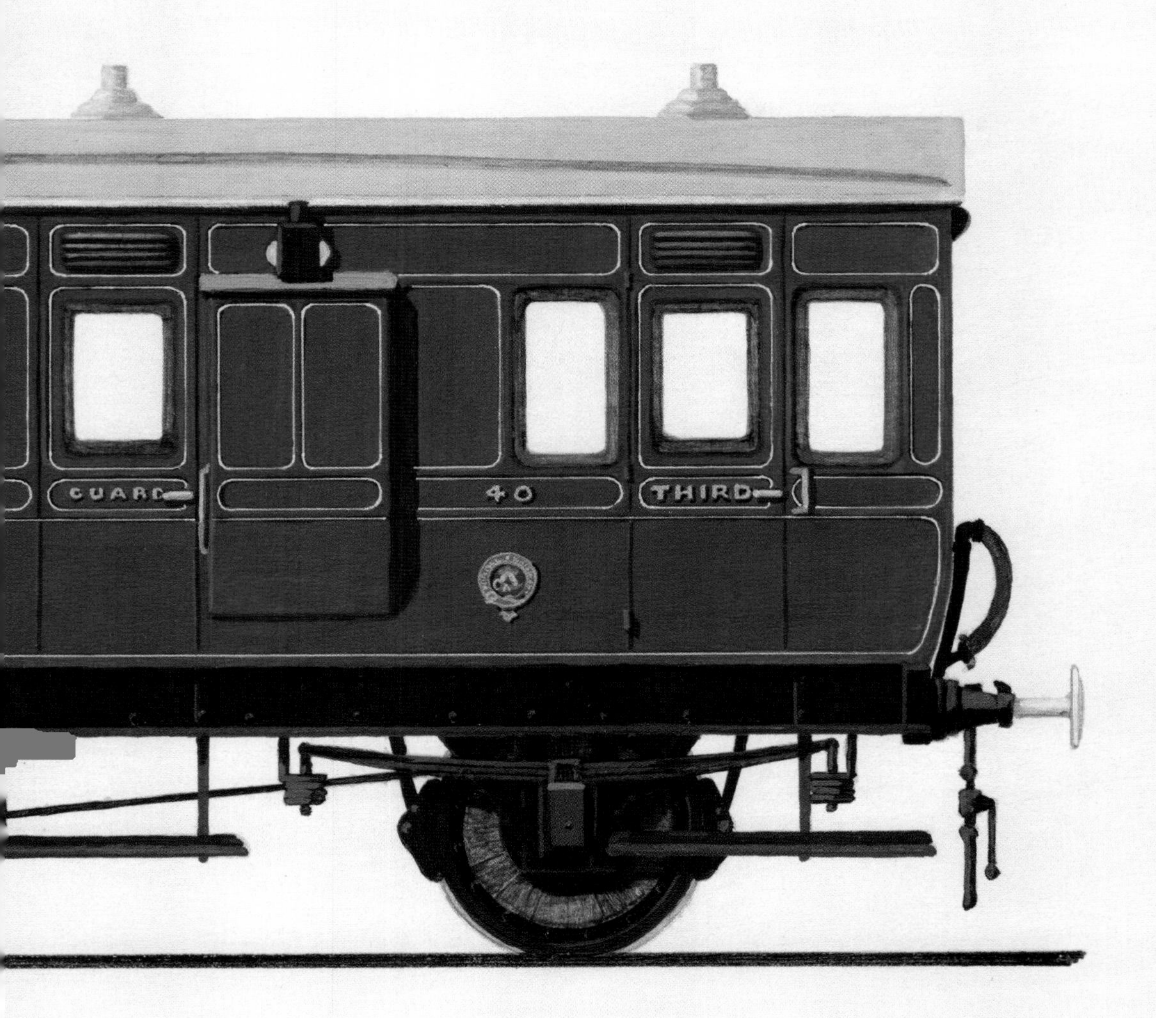

to class marking in words on each door and the numbers, two to each side. Characters were yellow, shaded in black. Below each number was the Wirral device, the only sign of ownership. Brake ends were painted vermilion.

There are insufficient photographs on which to base further details, except to say that roofs appear to have been painted grey, quickly deteriorating to black. Underframes were not lined and were reportedly painted black. There is another printed description of a carriage livery somewhat different from the above, but this seems to be of Mersey Railway stock, which before electrification worked through onto the WR.

Wagons, of which there were 118 of various types in 1908, were painted grey. The grey was reported as 'light', but does not appear particularly light on those few photographs that show any WR wagons. Ends of goods brake vans were painted vermilion. Lettering was in white, featuring a large "W R" in bold characters. This was about 18 inches high on most stock, but where space was restricted, for instance on low-sided open wagons, the size was reduced to about 12 inches. On the solebar was an elliptical numberplate with the number central, "WIRRAL" over it and "RAILWAY" underneath.

Wagon sheets had no distinguishing marks and were reportedly simply lettered "W.R.", presumably with the sheet number.

1 'Vermilion'
Carter 36
Pantone 485
BS 5252 04 E 55
or BS 381 536
'Poppy Red'

2 'Crimson Lake'
Carter 28
Pantone 188
BS 381 540 'Crimson'

Wrexham, Mold & Connah's Quay Railway

The Wrexham district in the north-east corner of Wales was the location of considerable numbers of coal pits, brick works and potteries, but the major railway companies such as the Great Western and the London & North Western skirted around the area. Local industries needed independent rail access to shipping on the Dee estuary and to the main line railways. In this spirit, the Buckley Railway was incorporated in 1860. This five-mile line was opened for mineral traffic only from Buckley (north of Wrexham) to the small Dee port of Connah's Quay in 1862.

Also in 1862, the Wrexham, Mold & Connah's Quay Junction Railway was incorporated for a line from Wrexham to join the Buckley Railway. This line was opened from Wrexham Exchange near the GWR station to Buckley in 1866. A junction was also formed with the L&NWR where the WM&CQ crossed it at Hope. A joint working agreement with the Buckley Railway was formed in July 1866 and it was finally vested in the WM&CQ in 1873.

The WM&CQ was always in financial difficulty and never seemed to be able to pay its officers or buy its locomotives. However, in 1881 Benjamin Piercy, the principal promotor and original engineer of the line returned to the district and resumed his interest in the WM&CQ. He encouraged the railway to expand, first by an extension from Wrexham Exchange to a new station at Wrexham Central (1887), secondly by a branch to Brymbo (opened for passengers in 1889) and then by a scheme to cross the Dee and reach Chester in partnership with the Manchester, Sheffield & Lincolnshire Railway. This last line, leaving the original alignment at Buckley Junction station, crossing the Dee at Hawarden Bridge and then joining a new MS&L line to Chester, was opened in 1890. A more ambitious and ultimately disastrous scheme was the Wirral Railways Joint Committee of 1885, in which a line was to be built from the Chester line at Hawarden Bridge to Bidston (near Birkenhead). The line was opened jointly with the MS&L as the North Wales & Liverpool Railway in 1896. WM&CQ trains ran to Seacombe, not being allowed onto the Mersey Railway as first planned.

However, the MS&L had advanced the money to the WM&CQ to build the line and it called in the debt. From 1897 the WM&CQ was controlled by a Receiver appointed by the MS&L, now known as the Great Central Railway. From this time the railway, although nominally still the WM&CQ, was operated as a satellite of the GCR. Finally, from 1st January 1905 it was absorbed completely.

As part of the Great Central, the WM&CQ was absorbed into the London & North Eastern Railway in 1923, but on Nationalisation it was allocated to the London Midland Region of British Railways.

The WM&CQ is one of those railways that have had very little written about their liveries. It is only possible to present what is thought to be true at the moment and hope that much more research is done in the future, particularly regarding rolling stock.

The early livery of the locomotive stock, most of which consisted of saddle tanks, is indefinite. The first two 0-6-0STs were delivered to the Buckley Railway in 1861, and a similar two to the WM&CQ in 1866. The Buckley examples are reported as being painted 'maroon' and it is possible all four engines were. Certainly, when the only tender engine the line ever possessed, the 0-6-0 *Chancellor*, arrived in 1866 secondhand from the London & North Western Railway, its exceptional green finish was noted by the locals. This

WM&CQR No. 3 had been rebuilt several times since its construction in 1863 before attaining the 2-6-0T form seen here in 1899. It carries the later livery with black edging and a single orange-yellow line. *John Alsop collection*

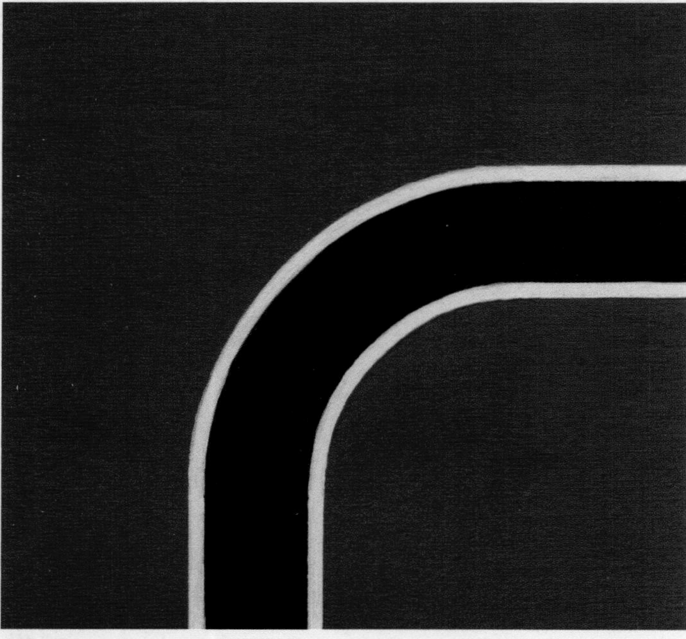

was almost certainly the standard Crewe green lined out in plain black.

All engines were named at first, the letters being applied to the tanks. The last engine to be named was No. 10 *Emily* of 1882. Subsequently numbers only were used. Numberplates were elliptical in brass, and usually had "WREXHAM MOLD AND" in small characters curving over the large seriffed central number, with "CONNAH'S QUAY RAILWAY" below. An exception to this was 0-4-0ST No. 11 of 1885, which had a small "Nº 11" on its plate. The background was vermilion.

By the 1890s, locomotives are reported as being painted Indian red [1]. It is possible that this may simply have been a more accurate name for the 'maroon' colour used from the 1860s. Lining was in black, fine-lined yellow in the conventional manner, forming panels on the cabs and saddletanks. Boiler bands, where visible, were black edged in yellow. There are few clear photographs, but it seems that wheel tyres were black, lined on their inner edge with yellow, and that axle ends were also black, ringed in yellow. Any splashers over the driving wheels, such as on No. 12, were edged

LEFT: Original engine lining.

with black and lined in yellow. The lower edge of the valance and the steps were similarly treated. Safety valves were polished brass, and some engines had polished copper chimney caps. There were no company markings, except for the numberplates. Bufferbeams were vermilion [2], edged with black and yellow, and the engine numbers appeared thereon in gold seriffed characters shaded in black, for example "N^{O} [hook] 12". Between the frames was also vermilion, rather clumsily called 'a crushed strawberry shade' in contemporary articles. Cab interiors are referred to as being cream.

Those few locomotives with side tanks were treated differently. Again photographs are rare, but No. 3 (1901), No. 5 (1884) and No. 8 (1880) all received the lettering "WM&CQ" and transferred numbers. Characters were in gold, shaded to right and below in blue and white. There may have been shadowing in black, but photos do not show it. No. 4 was rebuilt as a side tank engine in 1889, but the only published photo of it shows a brass numberplate and the armorial device transferred onto the tank over the leading wheel. Strangely, when No. 5 was rebuilt again in 1893, from an 0-6-0T to a 2-4-0T, an official view of it in photographic grey shows no lettering and a brass numberplate, but its appearance in traffic is not known.

From about 1896 much simpler lining was used on those few engines being painted. This reproduced the MS&LR style, having a broad black edging to body panels with a single orange-yellow line on the inside. This is the style applied to 2-6-0T No. 3, rebuilt at the WM&CQ's works at Rhosddu, and probably to the two 0-6-2Ts numbered 17 and 18, which were built for the WM&CQ by Beyer, Peacock, using a standard MS&L design. On the opening of the North Wales & Liverpool line several genuine MS&L engines were used, disguised for a year with WM&CQ letters and numbers 19 to 26 (almost certainly on MS&L green) until official running powers were granted.

In 1902 it is reported that 0-6-0ST No. 9 and 0-6-2ST No. 16 were painted black, having lining in Indian red edged in yellow. In this livery even the bufferbeams were painted black. It is suggested that black became the 'standard' livery of the line, but just how the small, impoverished works at Rhosddu could paint the entire stock of eighteen locomotives over a two year period is not specified. It is much more likely that these two and perhaps one or two other engines were the only examples, but to my mind the reversal of the colours suggests that the report may even be a misprint or error in proof-reading on behalf of the *Locomotive Magazine*.

When the GCR took over the WM&CQ, there were thirty-three carriages and one carriage truck on the books. The passenger vehicles were all 4-wheeled ex-L&NWR stock bought secondhand in the late 1880s. At first, carriages had retained their L&NWR livery; upper panels were 'flake white' [3] with lower panels and beading in dark purple brown [4]. Droplights were varnished wood and window mouldings were Venetian red. Before delivery, Crewe must have prepared the carriages, as on the opening of the Brymbo Branch it was noted that all five vehicles on the inaugural train had been newly-painted. This is probably too simplistic a viewpoint. It is far more likely that they would have been rubbed down, any "LNWR" transfers removed or painted over, then revarnished. From circa 1900 it is reported that carriages were being painted all-over dark brown as they went through the works, but as this was a slow process, many were still unchanged by 1905.

Details of lining and lettering are not recorded. Lining on the ex-L&NWR livery would have been yellow and white, but in the all-brown state it is likely there was no lining at all. Class marking was in words on each door. The original characters would have been gold outlined with black, but after repainting in brown it is probable that lettering was in yellow, possibly shaded with black. There appear to have been no company initials, faint traces on the well-known photo of a train at Brymbo suggesting that the armorial device was placed centrally on the lower panels, in the position where the former L&NWR script insignia would have been. Numbers and their positions are unknown.

Roofs would have been white originally, but it is unlikely they were touched by the WM&CQ, and so would have become grey or black over time. Solebars were probably black.

WM&CQR No. 2 was built for the Buckley Railway by Hudswell, Clarke in 1862 and had originally carried the name Kenyon. Although apparently unlined, close inspection shows traces on the bunker and cab of the later standard lining style.
John Alsop collection

WM&CQR No. 15, an 0-6-2ST built by Beyer, Peacock & Co. in 1888, at Brymbo station circa 1903. The company's fleet of 4-wheeled carriages were bought secondhand from the L&NWR and the second and third vehicles still retain their old livery.
John Alsop collection

Wrexham, Mold & Connah's Quay Railway

The wagons of the WM&CQ are another under-recorded subject. In 1905 there were 219 goods vehicles noted, but four of these could not be found. The colour is believed to have been grey. Markings are indefinite. Some wagons were lettered "W M & C Q R^{Y}" in small white letters spread along the sides in 1876, but the only wagon photographed in later times, grain wagon No. 24 of 1904, has just a solebar numberplate. This was rectangular with "W.M.&" over and "C.Q.R^{Y}" under the central number.

Wagon sheets were lettered with the initials "W.M.& C.Q.R." and the number, and in the middle of the sheet was a yellow right-angled cross, as opposed to one painted on the diagonal.

Long Life to Railway equipment

ONLY by protecting and preserving the paintable surfaces with materials specially designed to withstand the severe exposure and the strain and tension of traction—which disintegrate ordinary paints and varnishes—can this long life be *economically* achieved. Here are a few of the Berger Specialities designed for the purpose—and guaranteed by our 153 years' reputation :—

Berger's Mail Red and Scarlet—Two strong permanent reds much used for signals and brake vans.

Berger's "Metalac"—A metal protective paint, made of graphite of 93 per cent. purity—gives unequalled preservation to all structural steel work, bridges, etc.

Berger's Bogie Paint — for under-carriages.

Berger's Standard Station Paint—The highest-grade oil paint made—for inside and outside of station buildings.

Berger's Free-flowing Varnish-gloss Colours—Produce a "varnish finish" on coaches, without the use of varnish—saving labour, time and material.

Berger's Ready-bound Coach Colours—Give the finest coach finish (under varnish) it is possible to obtain.

Berger's "Berjapan"—A high-grade finishing varnish paint.

Berger's "Enamelac"—The highest-grade of enamel paint made. In white or colours.

Berger's Varnishes—Special products for specific railway work, all designed to give utmost durability.

A valuable text book on Railway Painting, showing colour patterns, sent free on request to Railway Engineers, Storekeepers, Carriage and Wagon Superintendents, etc., interested in

Berger's Paints, Colours and Varnishes

for Railway Work.

Lewis Berger & Sons, Ltd.,
Makers of Paints, Colours and Varnishes,
HOMERTON, LONDON, N.E.
Branches : Liverpool, Paris, Dresden, Vienna, Copenhagen,
Sydney, Wellington, Bombay, Calcutta, New York.

Limerick Lace

A Social History
and
A Maker's Manual